CW01083224

SENIORS GUIDE TO iPad

A Complete Senior-Friendly Illustrated Guide to Master Your New iPad. Learn Everything, from the Basics to the More Advanced Stuff, Without Complex Technical Jargon

Michael C. Harris

Copyright - 2020 - All rights reserved.

The content contained within this book may not be reproduced, duplicated or transmitted without direct written permission from the author or the publisher.

Under no circumstances will any blame or legal responsibility be held against the publisher, or author, for any damages, reparation, or monetary loss due to the information contained within this book. Either directly or indirectly.

Legal Notice:

This book is copyright protected. This book is only for personal use. You cannot amend, distribute, sell, use, quote or paraphrase any part, or the content within this book, without the consent of the author or publisher.

Disclaimer Notice:

Please note the information contained within this document is for educational and entertainment purposes only. All effort has been executed to present accurate, up to date, and reliable, complete information. No warranties of any kind are declared or implied. Readers acknowledge that the author is not engaging in the rendering of legal, financial, medical or professional advice. The content within this book has been derived from various sources. Please consult a licensed professional before attempting any techniques outlined in this book.

By reading this document, the reader agrees that under no circumstances is the author responsible for any losses, direct or indirect, which are incurred as a result of the use of information contained within this document, including, but not limited to, - errors, omissions, or inaccuracies.

AirDrop, AirMac, AirPlay, AirPods, AirPort, AirTunes, Apple ProRes, Apple Remote Desktop, AppleScript Studio, Apple Studio Display, AppleVision, Apple Watch Edition, Apple Watch Sport, FaceTime, Final Cut Studio, iBooks, iCal, iChat, iMac, iMovie, iPad, iPhone, iPod, iTunes, MacBook, MacBook Air, OS X, QuickTime, Safari, Time Machine **are trademarks of Apple inc.**, registered in the U.S. and other countries.

TABLE OF CONTENTS

INTRODUCTION

Steve Jobs, Apple's founder, and then CEO, announced the "iPad" at an Apple press conference in San Francisco on January 27, 2010. Because of the versatility and portability, it provides for consumers, the iPad's announcement is a watershed moment in modern technology. Steve Jobs was always fascinated by computers, and he was irritated that tablets were less efficient than modern computers.

Jobs began to advance Apple's technology in the 1990s with the goal of making it usable by hand and capable of providing a great and unique experience to the end-user. The Newton MessagePad, PowerBook Duo, and MessagePad 2100 were early iPad pioneers that received little public attention. They were discontinued shortly after their respective launches due to a lack of sales, forcing Steve Jobs to put an end to his tablet experimentation for a short time.

However, the future of a brand new Apple tablet became possible when Steve Jobs announced to the world in 2007 a modern new device called the "iPhone." The iPhone also pioneered the use of a touch screen, which was revolutionary in the technological world at the time.

With the massive success of the iPhone in 2007, Steve Jobs acquired enough capital for his tablet ideas to become a real product, and by 2009, rumors about Apple's new tablet were spreading all over public forums on the internet. The hype was genuine. People were ecstatic that their tablets could serve as reading, entertainment, and communication device while fitting in their palms. The iPad has been a huge success as a digital product since its debut. Apple sold over three million iPads in less than 90 days after they became available. Long lines formed in front of Apple stores to obtain this next technological innovation, which would later become one of the most popular portable tablets in history.

Apple had sold more than 15 million iPads by the time the next generation iPad 2 was released, making it the most popular tablet on the market. iPads have not lost their allure since their inception, but they have advanced in technology and become great portable devices for a wide range of demographics. Modern iPads have a plethora of applications and are visually appealing. Apple's iPad research team has made certain that they provide value to as many people as possible. This guidebook will help all seniors to get started with their new Ipad. Let's get started.

CHAPTER 1
YOUR NEW IPAD

The iPad is a popular technological device that has revolutionized itself in the last ten years. With a few clicks, you can read books, watch music, play videos, do office work, or turn your iPad into a gaming machine. You may have seen the long lines outside the Apple store whenever an iPad is released. iPads are always in high demand. Apple has reported selling three times as many devices as the previous year, particularly during the lockdown.

Purchasing an iPad can be a daunting decision because a significant amount of money must be invested, and there are numerous iPads on the market right now, making it difficult for an individual to determine which one is best for them.

Which iPad Should You Buy?

Regardless of how many recommendations you consider, it would be beneficial if you eventually decided on an iPad that meets your needs. Different iPad models serve different purposes and target different customer demographics. Remember that, while the hardware on these models varies, they all run the same iPad OS. As a result, you don't have to worry about incompatible apps when using a low-end iPad. It is important to note, however, that the Pro models offer some additional software enhancements to device owners.

Before purchasing an iPad, you should assess your needs using four criteria.

The display of the iPad is a major factor in deciding which iPad to purchase. All iPad Pro models have higher-quality screens than the competition, making them a better choice for professionals and those who value aesthetics. Except for the Pro-motion technology, which is exclusive to pro models, the next-generation iPad Air models have excellent displays. iPad Mini models typically have the same Liquid Retina display as iPad Air models, but with smaller screen sizes.

Basic iPad models have significantly lower resolution, brightness, and lack a laminated display. However, for the price, they still have an excellent retina display.

While we obviously leave the decision on which iPad model to buy entirely up to you, we do want to make some suggestions.

iPad Pro models are ideal for digital artists, professionals, and those who require higher visual contrast.

Models of iPad Air that Are Best for Everyone

iPad Mini models are ideal for those who prefer small screens.

If you want to choose an iPad based on screen size, get the basic iPad:

» 12.9-inch screens: For those who struggle to read text on small screens.
» 10.9-inch screens: These are ideal for all users who require large text.
» iPad mini for reading.
» If you have a visual impairment, either the iPad Pro or iPad Air models are recommended. They have a wide color display, allowing you to interact with the screens without straining your eyes.

Processing Power

Processing power is another critical factor you need to consider before purchasing an iPad. All new iPad models, irrespective of price, can handle complex tasks. However, if you are a user who needs high graphical power and needs an advanced Neural engine, then the new iPad Pro model that comes with an Apple M1 chip is the best choice for you. Newer iPad Pro models can also be bought with either 8 Gigabytes (GB) RAM or 16GB RAM.

If You Want to Choose an iPad Based on Usage

» Light user: iPad Basic model (6th generation and above)
» Complex tasks: iPad Pro models and iPad mini
» Best for everyone: New iPad Air models with an A14 Bionic Chip

Storage

Many users nowadays depend on cloud storage to meet their storage needs. However, if you are an iPad user who needs a lot of storage, choosing the pro models is a better option because you can get storage up to 2 Terabytes (TB) with the newer iPad Pro models. Basic iPads start with 64 GB making them insufficient for many users.

If you want to choose an iPad based on storage requirements:

» iPad Pro models: For people with a memory requirement of more than 256 GB

» iPad Air models: For people with a memory requirement of more than 64 GB and less than 256 GB

» iPad Basic models: For light users with less memory requirement

Network Connection

All iPad models come with two different variants based on network communication.

1. Wi-Fi models are great for people who stay indoors most of the time and don't need to travel a lot.

2. Wi-Fi + Cellular models are great for people who travel a lot with their devices.

Once you have decided which iPad to choose, reach out to your nearest Apple store or order from the official website. Several payment options such as Apple Pay, Google Pay, credit, and debit cards are available for ordering an iPad of your choice either on the website or in the store.

CHAPTER 2
FIRST TIME WITH YOUR IPAD

When you turn on your iPad for the first time, you will be asked to select some settings like selected language, Wi-Fi network, Apple ID, and more. You don't have to answer all these many questions when you are setting up. You can skip some of them now and change them later.

After opening the iPad from its box, click and hold the power button to turn it on. Wait for the operating system (OS) to finish booting, and then follow these steps:

1. Please select the language of the operating system. Most third-party applications you install will also reflect this language setting.

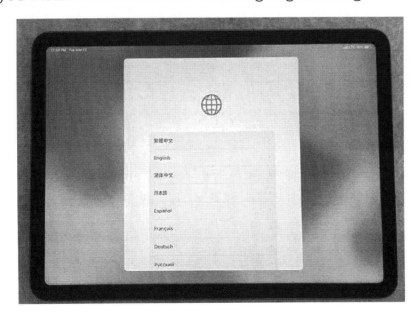

2. Please select your region or country. This will adjust the service and features accordingly.

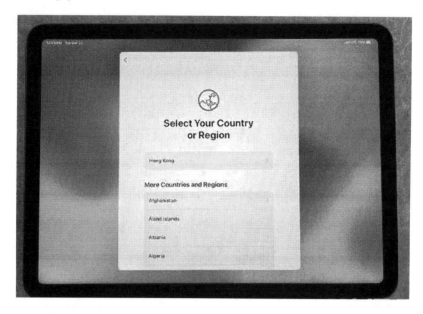

3. If you have another iOS / iPad operating system, you can move it closer to the new iPad to transfer data quickly. Otherwise, click Manually Adjust to start from scratch.

4. Please check your language setting. You can make all the necessary changes by clicking on Customize settings.

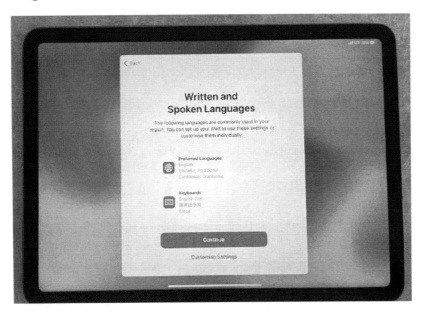

5. The Preferred Language setting allows you to select the priority of the spoken language. For example, if your app does not support English, it is by default a traditional Chinese language.

6. Select the language you want to add to your iPad keyboard and click Continue.

7. Dictating allows you to turn your speech into text. Select the language you use in Dictation and click Continue.

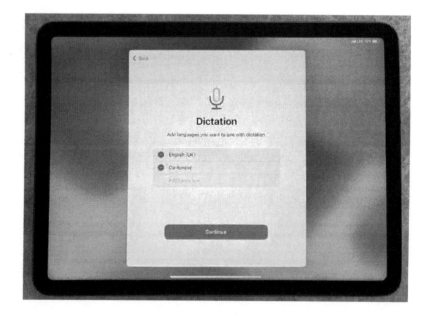

8. Click on your name and enter your password to connect to your Wi-Fi home network. An Internet connection is required to complete the installation process and take advantage of the features that come with the iPad OS.

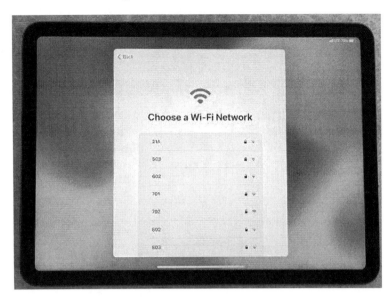

9. It can take up to a few minutes for your iPad to connect and activate your Apple server. This is to make sure you have not been robbed and start counting down the warranty that comes with it.

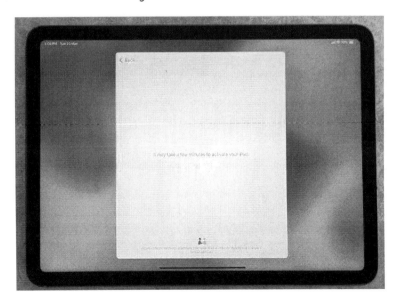

10. Carefully read Apple's data and privacy policy and click Continue.

11. Set Touch ID as an option. This allows you to unlock the iPad by placing your finger on the power button.

12. To set the Touch ID, release the switch repeatedly with your finger to record your fingerprint.

13. After setting up Touch ID, you need to select a password as a security measure. You can change your passcode from a numeric passcode to an alphanumeric password using the Password Options button. Once you have determined the type of password, enter it twice to confirm it.

14. Decide whether to restore your cloud or local backup from another device. Alternatively, you can click Do not transfer applications and data to start from scratch.

15. Sign in to your Apple ID to access company features like iMessage, FaceTime, and App Store downloads.

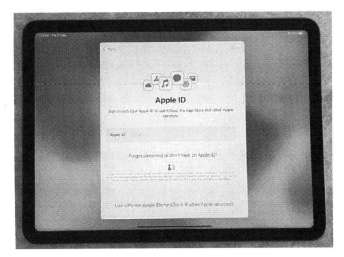

16. Please read the Terms of Use carefully and click [Agree] if you agree. If you do not agree, you will not be able to use the new iPad.

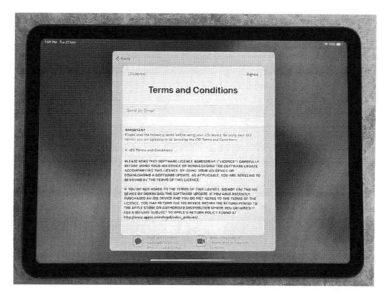

17. Click Continue to get automatic iPad OS software updates in the future. You can disable this option later in normal settings.

18. If necessary, enable location services to help your app provide more accurate information and use navigation services and maps.

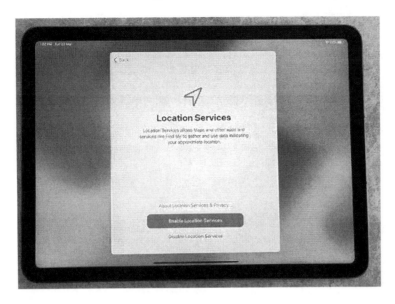

19. If you like, you can enable Siri, a virtual assistant. Siri can answer your questions, perform tasks and provide relevant information in a timely manner.

20. If you enable Siri, decide which language you want Siri to use.

21. Select the sound you want to use with Siri. The included voice has different emphases and human characteristics, so you can choose the voice that suits you.

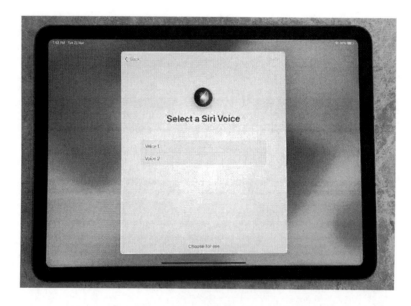

22. Activate Hey Siri if necessary. This allows you to call Siri hands-free by saying Hey Siri.

23. Choose whether Apple should collect audio recordings to improve Siri. If you decide to share them, your data will be anonymous and will not be linked to your credentials.

24. Screen time monitors the time spent on iPad and sets optional limits and child supervision. You can optionally click Continue to enable this feature.

25. Apple collects anonymous logs from your iPad and which it uses to improve its products and services. You can choose to allow or block this.

26. Decide if you want to use your iPad in light or dark mode. You can later select the automatic option in the display settings. Dark mode adds a gray/black background to the system and supported apps and light mode makes it a lighter color like white.

27. Click Getting Started to get started with iPad.

Congratulations!

Screen Gestures

Gestures, sometimes called multi-touch gestures, are used to open apps and browse the web.

Tap, touch and hold, swipe, scroll, and zoom are all simple gestures.

- » Tap: One finger lightly touches the screen.
- » Hold down the button: To preview the content in response, press and hold an item in the application. To open the shortcut menu, press and hold the application icon on the Home screen for a few seconds.
- » Swipe: Quickly move one finger across the screen.
- » Scroll: Move one finger across the screen without lifting your finger. In the Photos app, for example, you can scroll through a list by dragging it up or down to see more pictures. Swipe to quickly scroll. Touch the screen to stop scrolling.

» Zoom: Put two fingers near each other on the screen. Spread them apart to enlarge, or bring them together to zoom out.
» You can also double-tap an image or webpage to enlarge, or tap twice again for further zooming.
» On the map app, double-click, hold and drag up to zoom in, or drag down to zoom out.

(*Advanced Gestures*)

Go home. You can return to the home screen at any time by swiping from the bottom of the screen. See Opening apps on iPad.

Quickly open controls. Swipe down from the upper right edge of the screen to access the control panel. If you'd like to see more options, hold the control. See Using and Customizing the Control Panel on the iPad.

Open the application switcher. Swipe up from the bottom edge, pause when you get to the center of the screen, and then lift your finger. To look through open applications, swipe right, and then tap the application you want to use. See Switch apps on iPad.

Switch between open applications. Swipe left or right along the bottom edge of the screen to quickly switch between open applications. See Switch between iPad applications.

Open the Dock while inside an app. Swipe up from the bottom edge of the screen to pause and highlight Dock. To open another application quickly, click on the app in Dock.

Take a screenshot. Press and release the top button and one of the volume keys at the same time.

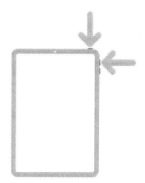

Switch off. Hold down the top button and one of the volume keys at the same time until you see the slider, then drag the top slider to turn it off.

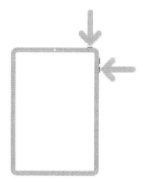

Force restart. Press and hold the volume key next to the top button, press and release the other volume key quickly, and press and hold the top key until you see the Apple logo. Three steps, a little tricky, but once you master it, it becomes easy.

Virtual Keyboard

The iPad includes a virtual keyboard that can be used to enter text into the device. You can purchase a physical keyboard for your iPad. But that may not be necessary because the iPad's virtual keyboard includes everything you'll need, as well as shortcuts to make typing easier.

To Access the Keyboard: When you tap a text box, the iPad virtual keyboard appears. When writing an email, leaving a comment, or entering a web address, for example, you will see the keyboard.

Understanding the Keyboard

There are several keys and features on the keyboard that you should be aware of. Some examples are:

» Cursor: The cursor indicates the location of the text.
» Backspace Button: Tap the Backspace key to delete the letters to the left of the cursor. To delete the entire word, press and hold the Backspace key.

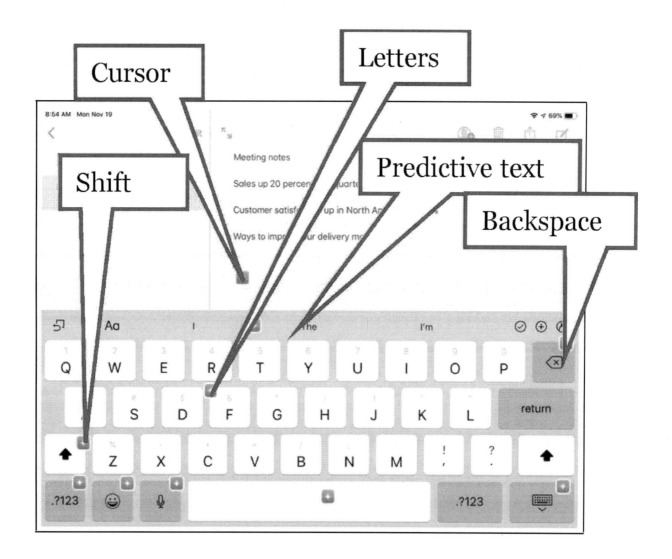

Cursor

Letters

Shift

Predictive text

Backspace

Predictive Text

iPad will create automated text based on what you're writing and what you've written in the past. Click on a word to enter it.

Hide Keyboard

Click here to hide the keyboard. You can display the keyboard again by clicking on any text box.

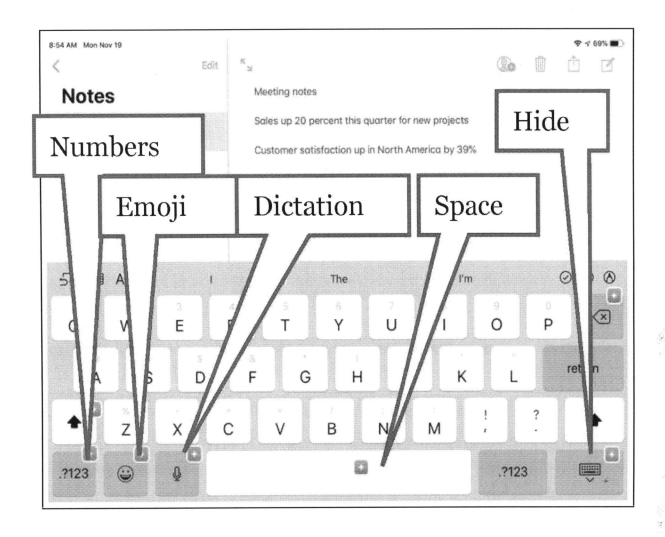

The Space Bar

To insert a space, press the space bar. When you double-click a space at the end of a sentence, it automatically adds a full stop.

Dictation by Voice

You can use this feature to create a text simply by speaking instead of typing on the keyboard. To begin speaking, press the microphone icon on your keyboard.

Keyboard Emoji

To change your keyboard from text to emoji, tap here: Functions of the Keyboard.

Several features of the iPad Virtual Keyboard make typing into your device faster and easier.

Suggestion:

As you type, the iPad suggests special words. You can use suggestions while writing by simply tapping the space bar. In the following example, we used the proposal to change agreem to agreement. To reject a proposal, disregard it and

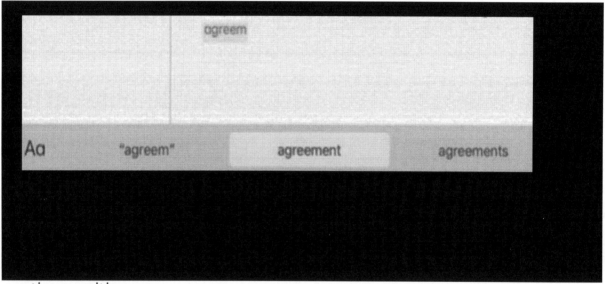

continue writing.

Automatic Correction

iPad will automatically correct common spelling errors. For example, teh will be converted to the. This is a powerful feature, but auto-correction is not perfect. It's also automatic so you don't always notice when something changes. You should always check the text to make sure it is correct.

Error Search

In addition to automatic correction, iPad detects spelling errors as you type. Words with spelling errors are underlined in red. Tap words to see suggestions for possible spelling mistakes. A list of possible spellings is displayed. You can replace the existing word by simply clicking on the suggestion.

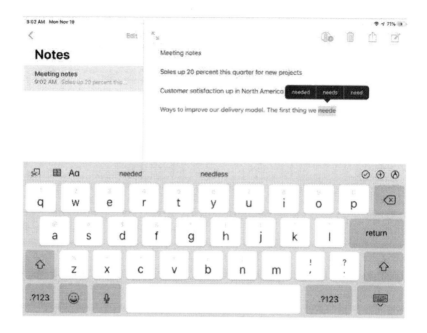

Move The Cursor

Sometimes you want to change something at the beginning of a sentence or paragraph. Instead of deleting existing text and starting over, you can move the cursor to the desired location. To move the cursor, just tap on the desired location.

If you need more control, hold down the screen and then drag the magnifying glass (without releasing your finger), to select the cursor.

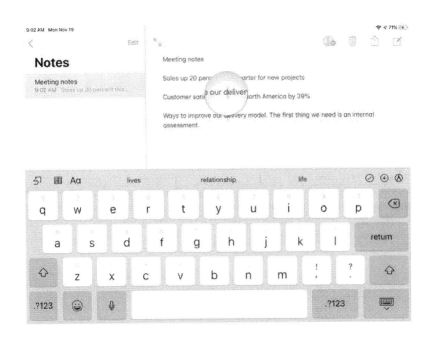

To Copy and Paste the Text

If you want to move the text from one place to another, you can copy and paste it. This is especially useful when transferring text between different applications. For example, you can find useful information in Safari, copy it and paste it into your Notes app.

First, you need to select the text you want to copy. Double-click the screen next to the text you want to select and drag the selection handle to select the text.

Menu options such as cut, copy and paste appear above the selected text. Tap Copy.

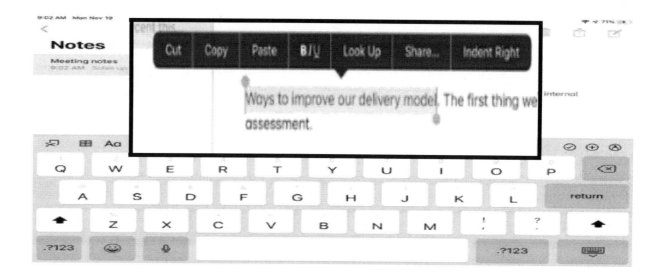

Double-tap the desired place in the text, then tap Paste.

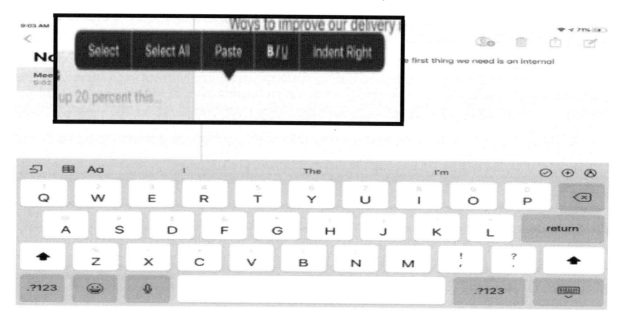

The copied text is displayed.

How to Use the Control Center

The Control Center provides quick access to brightness, volume, camera, cellular data, airplane mode, Wi-Fi, AirDrop, screen orientation, and other important features.

Swipe down from the top-right corner of the screen to access the control center. To close it, swipe up from the bottom of the screen or simply click anywhere on the screen.

CHAPTER 3
IPAD APP STORE AND APPS

How to Create a Gmail Account

Use the Mail Application

You can use it to view and send emails, reply to messages, manage your inbox and much more than you are used to doing with your email account.

The first time you open the email application, you need to connect to your current email address. Select your email provider and follow the instructions to link your account to the email application. When done, you will be able to send and receive emails from that account on your iPad.

Add Another Email Account

If you use multiple email accounts (for example, for personal email and for work email), you can add multiple accounts to your email application. This allows you to manage all your messages in one place.

» To add another email account, from the Home screen, tap the Settings icon.

» Tap Passwords & Accounts in the left panel, and then select Add Account. Follow the instructions to link your new account.

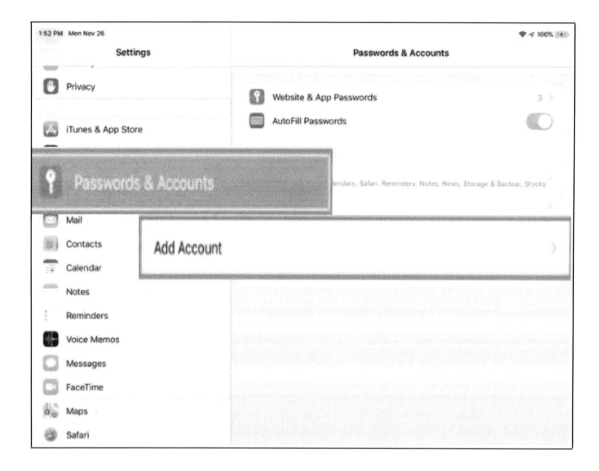

Notification Via Email

A sign will appear on the app icon when you receive a new email. This figure indicates the number of unread emails in your inbox. This allows you to search for new messages without opening the Mail app.

Go to Settings, click Notification Center, and then select Email to customize your notifications.

Gesture of Swiping

Folders and flags are two useful tools in the Mail app for managing your mailbox. Swipe left on the message to access options like Archive or delete, reply and forward.

Personalize Your Email Signature

Each email you send by default includes the phrase "sent from iPad" at the bottom of the message. This is the e-mail application's default e-mail signature. Open Settings from the Home screen, tap Email in the left pane and then select Signature to customize or delete your email signature.

How to Install Apps

Even if you are new to the iPad, you have most likely heard of the app (short for application). The concept is straightforward. A computer program designed to run on your device is known as an application. The iPad comes with a few pre-installed apps, but you can get more from the App Store. The iPad also makes it simple to manage applications on your device.

App Store

The App Store gives you access to hundreds of thousands of apps. From games to entertainment to productivity tools, you'll find everything from apps to help with common tasks like studying for exams, cooking dinners, and monitoring itineraries.

You're going to find countless free apps that can be downloaded for free. Many others cost only $ 0.99, but some are more expensive. If you are not sure which app to try first, you can choose from suggestions in the App Store or view apps that are popular with other iPad users.

What Makes Up the App Store?

Some features that you'll find in the app store are shown in the diagram below:

- » Account: Change account options, view purchased apps, used gift cards, and more in the Account menu.
- » Today: The tab is now updated daily with the most recent apps and games, as well as articles from the App Store editor.
- » Game: The Games tab contains a variety of games that can be downloaded to your iPad. Non-game applications are housed in the application section. They are organized into viewable categories.
- » Update: All of the updates for the applications on your iPad can be found here.
- » Search: To find your application, go to the Search tab.
- » To purchase apps (including free apps) from the App Store, you must have an Apple ID and a valid credit card.
- » Visit The App Store: When you first visit the App Store, you will see a variety of new apps and games to try out. If you're looking for something specific, click the Apps button to navigate to the category you're looking for.
- » Each category contains a list of popular applications. Each app keeps track of its cost (or says Get if it's free). You can view the data by clicking on the app. The app page displays data about the app's behavior, user reviews, screenshots, and other information.
- » Multitasking: You may be accustomed to running multiple programs on your computer at once. This is also referred to as multitasking. Multitasking on the iPad is a little different. You cannot use multiple applications at the same time, but you can easily switch between them without returning to the home screen.

The iPad will continue to pause recent apps in the background to make multitasking as seamless as possible. You will not have to wait for the app to load again if you switch to a recent app. Simply resume where you left off.

To Change Applications

You might want to quickly switch between applications without returning to the home screen. Assume you're using Safari to browse the Internet and decide to send an e-mail message.

Navigate to the application switcher. Swipe up from the bottom edge of the screen, pause when you reach the center, and then lift your finger.

A preview of the currently available applications is shown. To view current applications, swipe left or right. Simply tap the app to open it.

To Close the App

Even if you return to the home screen, the app you're using does not truly close. Instead, it is in the background in standby mode. However, if the app does not function properly, it may assist in forcing the app to close. This is analogous to terminating a program that isn't responding to your computer.

It is important to note that unless you are experiencing problems, you do not need to close the app in this manner. Because the apps are paused, your iPad will not slow down or drain its battery.

Swipe up from the bottom edge of the screen, pause when you reach the center, and then lift your finger.

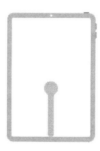

A preview of the current application is displayed. Swipe the app up to close it.

Manage Applications

The home screen contains icons for all of your device's applications. This means it can get quite crowded, especially if you've downloaded a lot of apps from the App Store. Here are some tips for customizing your home screen so you can quickly find your favorite apps.

» Press and hold an application on the home screen to rearrange the icons. When the icon begins to shake, drag and drop it wherever you want (whether inside or outside the dock). To move the icon to another screen, drag it to the left or right edge and press and hold until the screen changes. Swipe up from the bottom of the screen when finished to prevent the icons from shaking.

» If you're on the last page of your app, you can drag the icon to the far right to create more home screens.

Once you finish swipe up from the bottom of the screen.

» Create a folder: Drag one icon to another to create a folder. Keep dragging and dropping the necessary icons to add them to the folder. This is a great way to organize similar apps and get rid of clutter from your home screen.

Once you finish go to the home screen. You can return to the home screen at any time by swiping from the bottom of the screen.

» Search for apps: Swipe right from the middle of the Home screen to search for applications. A search box will pop up at the up of the screen. When you start typing the name of the app you want, the apps that match your search will appear (along with other files and settings on the iPad).

» Delete apps: From the Home screen, press and hold the app, then tap the X in the upper left corner to remove the app.

» Once you finish, swipe up from the bottom of the screen.

App Updates

Over time, many applications receive updates from app developers. Updates usually help make your program smoother and can introduce new features.

By default, iPad will automatically download these updates. However, you can disable this feature if you want to update the app manually. If automatic updates are turned off, a notification bar will appear on the App Store icon when updates are available for any of the installed applications.

To Change Auto-Update Settings

If desired, you can configure your iPad to install all updates automatically.

» From the Home screen, tap the Settings icon.

» Tap iTunes & App Store, then click Update to turn automatic updates on or off.

To Update the Application Manually

Open the App Store and click on Updates. A list of available updates is displayed. Tap Update to update the application. You can also click on Update all to install all available updates.

1:36 PM   Mon Nov 19   📶 🔋 100% 🔋

Updates

Pending

 Paper by WeTransfer
Nov 13, 2018   UPDATE

 Update All

SM **Meraki Syste**
Jul 14, 2018

This update implements the new double tap gesture for Apple
Pencil 2.   more

Minor update to fix minor issues   more

 FontBook™ Typef
Nov 3, 2017

 UPDATE

• added iPhone X support
• minor improvements   more

 Today   Games   Apps   Updates   Search

CHAPTER 4
NETWORK AND COMMUNICATION

A lot of what an iPad can do requires an Internet connection. Sending and receiving emails, searching for information, video chatting via Face-Time, viewing streaming videos, and listening to streaming music all require an Internet connection.

To connect your iPad to the Internet, you use a Wi-Fi wireless connection. Because your iPad has built-in Wi-Fi, all you need to do is connect to a private Wi-Fi network (such as your home network) or a public Wi-Fi hotspot. Once connected, you can do all of the wonderful Internet-related things you want, as well as use the applications that require an Internet connection.

How to Join a Wi-Fi Network

You'll need to connect your iPad to the Internet over a wireless network to get the most out of it. You can also use your home Wi-Fi network or a public Wi-Fi network or hotspot to connect.

Connect to Your Wireless Network at Home

Connect your iPad to your home wireless network if you have one. After connecting the first time, you won't have to reconnect manually again; your iPad remembers the network settings and reconnects automatically.

To connect to your home network, you'll need to know the network name (also known as an SSID, or service set identifier) and the network password (sometimes called a security key).

Following are the steps:

» Tap the Settings icon to access the Settings page.
» Wi-Fi can be found in the left column. (Note: If you aren't yet connected, it should say "Not Connected").
» Make sure the Wi-Fi switch is turned on. Touch to turn it on if it isn't already.
» A list of nearby wireless networks appears. Tap to select your home network. As a result of this action, the password panel appears.
» Using the onscreen keyboard, enter the password for your network.
» Click the Join button. (Note: You will now be connected to the network and have access to the Internet.)

Current Wi-Fi Network Connection

If you're currently connected to a wireless network, the name of that network appears in the Wi-Fi field in the left column of the Wi-Fi page. You can connect to a different network if you want.

How to Use a Public Wireless Hotspot

Most wireless networks and hotspots in the real world are public networks, which means you don't need a password to join. Simply select the network from the list and click Connect. (Note: You're connected if the Wi-Fi symbol appears in the status bar at the top of the screen.)

Some public networks, on the other hand, require you to read and agree to their terms of service after connecting but before using the network.

In this case, your web browser will typically display a connection page. (In some cases, you may need to manually launch the Safari browser and view a web page before the wireless connection screen appears.) When viewing the connection page from the wireless network or hotspot, you may need to select an "I read that" option or click a "connect" button.

You must manually log in to your local Starbucks or McDonald's wireless networks, for example, using their log-in sites. In some cases, there may be a fee to access the wireless network, in which case you must provide your credit card information to proceed.

Hotel Internet Access

When connecting to a wireless network at a hotel that does not offer free Wi-Fi, you typically enter your room number to have the charges added to your bill. Given that some hotels charge $10 or more per night for Wi-Fi, looking for hotels that provide it for free is always a good idea.

Touch Wi-Fi in the left column of the Settings screen.

Make sure the Wi-Fi switch is turned on. (Note: If it isn't already turned on, touch it to turn it on.)

There is a list of nearby wifi networks and hotspots. Tap to select the appropriate network.

If you are asked to sign in, the hotspot should launch the Safari browser and take you to a sign-in page. (Note: If this does not happen automatically, you may need to run Safari manually and then type any web page URL to get to the sign-in page.) Check the box next to any terms and conditions, then click the "accept" or "sign-in" button.

How to Switch Networks

You may have multiple Wi-Fi networks available to you, especially if you're out in public, and your iPad may connect to one that isn't the one you intended. If this is the case, switching networks is straightforward.

Look for the Wi-Fi field in the left column of the Settings screen. It displays the network to which you are currently connected. If you don't want to connect to this network, tap the Wi-Fi field to get a list of other available networks.

Choose the network to which you want to connect. (Note: Your iPad will be disconnected from the previous network and connected to the one you just selected.)

Connect to a Network to Which You've Already Been Linked

This one is considerably easier. When you come within range of a previously connected wireless network or hotspot, your iPad automatically reconnects. You don't have to select it from a list; the iPad will automatically detect and connect to the network.

When you're connected to a private network, such as your home network, your iPad remembers and enters your password for you. If you're using a public network or hotspot that requires you to sign in via your web browser, you may be prompted to agree to the terms and click the "sign-in" button again. (NB: You may not; some sites allow you to rejoin without entering your password again.)

It should be noted that not every Internet connection is dependable. Your iPad may be unable to connect to the Internet if the Wi-Fi network or hotspot you connect to has problems.

Similar connectivity issues may exist on your home Wi-Fi network. In many cases, the problem resolves itself in a matter of minutes. If the problem persists, try turning off and then on your iPad's Wi-Fi. This causes your iPad to connect to the wifi network or hotspot for the first time, which usually fixes the problem.

How to Browse Privately

There are some websites that you might want to visit in private and not tell anyone about. If you want to surf anonymously, use Safari's Private mode. Pages viewed in Private mode are not saved to your history or otherwise monitored on your device or elsewhere.

- » Open Safari and select the Tabs option.
- » Choose Private.
- » Click the Done button. You've activated private browsing mode.
- » In Safari, go about your business as usual. There will be no trace of you.
- » Tap the Tabs icon to exit private browsing mode.
- » Choose Private. (Note: Any tabs that were open prior to entering private browsing mode are now visible.)
- » Click the Done button.

How to Create a Contact

Click on the Contacts icon on the Home screen.

» The contacts list is displayed. Click on the + key above.

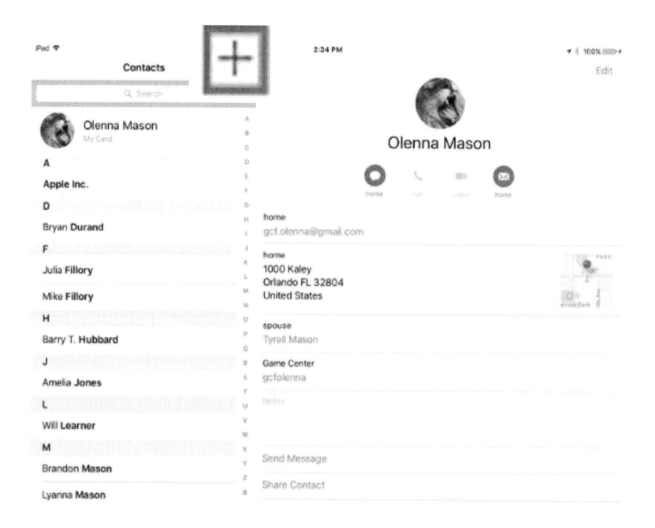

» Enter the relevant contact information. At the very least, you need to enter your 1st and last name and email address. However, you can also enter other information such as phone number, address and birthday.

» When you are finished, tap Done.
» To edit information for an existing contact, select the contact, and tap Edit.

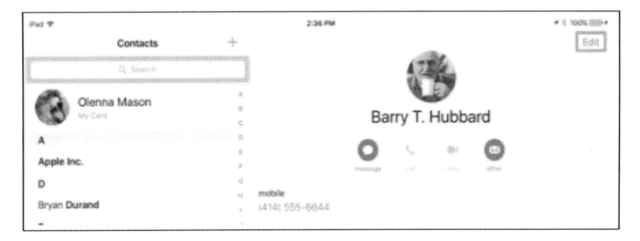

With FaceTime, you can connect with your friends & family, whether they are making use of an Apple device or not.

Make a FaceTime Call

To enter the application, click on the Settings application icon, then touch Face-Time and enable FaceTime.

Perform any of the following:

» Configure your account for FaceTime calls: Touch the Sign In button after selecting Use your Apple ID for FaceTime.
» In calls, share your display: Enable SharePlay by touching the SharePlay button.
» Take Live Photos while on a FaceTime call: Turn on FaceTime Live Photos.

Make A Link For FaceTime Calls

You can make a call link and send it to the people you want to join a FaceTime call with.

» In the FaceTime app, select the Create Link option.
» Choose one of the options for sending the link from the list (Message, Mail, etc.).

NB: Anyone, including those without Apple devices, can be invited to participate in the call. They can join the call using their browser without having to sign in.

Use Your iPad to Make FaceTime Calls

FaceTime calls can be made using an Apple ID and an Internet connection.

» Open the FaceTime app and tap the New FaceTime button.
» Enter the phone number or name of the person you want to call in the login field, and then tap the video or audio icon to initiate a FaceTime audio call.
» Alternatively, tap the Add Contact icon to launch the Contacts app and then begin your call, or tap a provided contact in your call history.

A Phone Call

When a FaceTime call comes in, do one of the following:

- » To accept the call, press the Accept button or move the slider.
- » To decline a call, click the Decline button.
- » Tap the Remind Me button to set a call-back reminder.
- » Send a text message to the caller by selecting the Message option.

Start a FaceTime Call From a Message Chat

You can initiate a call with the person with whom you are chatting in a Message chat.

- » In the upper right corner of the message conversation, tap the FaceTime icon.
- » Tap the FaceTime Audio or FaceTime Video buttons.

Remove a Phone Call From Your Call History

- » Swipe to the left on the call you want to delete in the FaceTime call history, then click the Delete button.

Take a FaceTime Live Photo

To take a live photo during a FaceTime call, first, make sure FaceTime Live Photos is enabled in the Settings app> FaceTime, then do any of the following:

- » During a one-on-one call, press the Capture button.
- » On a Group call, click on the person's tile, then tap the Full-Screen icon, followed by the Capture button.

Make a FaceTime Call as a Group

A FaceTime group call can have up to 32 participants.

- » In the FaceTime app, tap the New FaceTime button.
- » In the entry box, type the phone numbers or names of the people you intend to call.
- » Touch the Add Contacts icon to open the Contacts app and then add people, or tap a provided contact in your call history.
- » Tap the Video or Audio icons to initiate a video call or a FaceTime voice call.

Every caller would be displayed on a tile on your display. When the tile's participant begins speaking, the tile becomes more visible.

To prevent the speaker tile from expanding during a FaceTime Group call, open the Settings app, select FaceTime, and then disable Speaking in the Automatic Prominence section.

Add a Person to a Call

Everyone on the FaceTime call can invite others to join the call.

» During a FaceTime call, click on your screen to reveal the FaceTime controls (if you can't see them), then touch the top of the controls and then the Add Person button.
» In the login field, enter the person's name, phone number, or Apple ID.
» Select the Add People option.

Drop a Group Call

» To exit the group call, press the Leave button.
» The call would remain active if two or more people remained on the line.

In a FaceTime Call, Share Your Screen

FaceTime users can use the SharePlay feature to share their screens during a call, allowing them to bring websites, applications, and other media into the conversation.

» During a FaceTime call, touch your screen to reveal the FaceTime controls, then tap the Share Contents icon and then tap the Share My Screen button. After three seconds, your screen would appear in the FaceTime conversation.
» Press the Home Button to return to the Home Screen, then launch an app to share with those on the call.
» Click the Stop Content Sharing icon to stop sharing your display.

Enable the Center of Attention

While on a FaceTime call, the Center Stage feature allows your iPad's front-facing camera to automatically frame you as you move around the view field.

» Swipe down from the upper right corner of your screen to reveal the Controls Center while on a FaceTime call.

» Touch the Video Effects button, and then touch Center Stage to activate it.
» Touch Center Stage once more to turn it off.

Make Your Background Blur

» Portrait mode blurs your background and shifts the visual focus to you.
» In a FaceTime call, click on your tile.
» On your tile, click the Blur Background icon.
» To turn off portrait mode, click the Blur Background button again.

Use the Rear Camera

» Select your tile, then select the "Switch Camera" icon.
» Click on the Camera icon once more to use the front camera.

Turn Off Your Camera

» Click on your screen to see the controls then click on the Show Camera icon.

» Click on the button once more to turn on the camera.

iMessage

How Do You Send and Receive Messages?

To begin a conversation, open the messaging app and then click the compose icon. Next, enter a phone number or email address, or select a contact by clicking on the plus icon.

To resume a conversation, simply click on the conversation in the message list.

Go to settings and select General to use picture characters or emojis. Then, click on the keyboard, followed by "keyboards." Then, click "add new keyboard" and then "emoji" to enable the keyboard. Then, while typing a message, click on the globe icon to bring up the emoji keyboard.

Simply click on the contact at the top of the screen and then on the video icon to make a FaceTime call to the person you're texting.

To view a person's contact information, go to the top of the screen and click on the info icon.

To send a group message, click the compose icon and then enter the group's phone number(s) or email address(es).

To block unwanted messages, first, select the contact at the top of the screen, then select the info icon. Then, select "block this caller."

You can also block callers by going to settings, selecting FaceTime, and then "blocked."

Pay With Apple

Apple Pay can be used to make quick and secure payments in apps and on websites.

» Insert a Debit or Credit Card.
» To open the Settings app, click the icon, then select Wallet and Apple Pay.
» Select the Add Cards option.

Perform any of the following:

» Insert a new card: Insert your card information manually or position your iPad so that it is clearly visible in the frame on your screen.
» Add old cards: Select a card that has previously been used with your Apple ID or a card that has been removed. Click the Continue button and enter the card's CVV number.

View a Card's Information and Change Its Settings
» Go to the Settings app, then select Wallet and Apple Pay.
» Touch a card, then do any of the following:
» To view your history, tap Transaction.
» Take out the card.
» Examine the Device Account Number as well as the last four digits of the

card number.

» Make any necessary changes to the billing address.

Change Your Apple Pay Preferences

To open the Settings app, click the icon, then select Wallet and Apple Pay.

Perform any of the following:

» Enter your purchase and shipping information.
» Choose a default card.

Use Apple Pay to Make Payments

» Apple Pay can be used to make purchases in Application Clips, applications, and anywhere the Apple Pay button can be found online.
» Touch the Apple Pay button when checking out.
» Examine the payment information.
» You can change any of the specifics.
» Enter your passcode or use Touch ID to verify.

Set Up a Mail Account

To open the application, click the Settings app icon on your Home Screen, then select Mail> Account> Add Accounts.

Perform any of the following:

» Touch an e-mail service, such as Microsoft Exchange or iCloud, and enter the required information in the appropriate fields.
» Touch Others, then Add a Mail Account and fill out the form to create a new account.

Read an Email

» Touch the email you want to read from the mailbox.

Write an Email

Change mailboxes or accounts.

Delete, move, or mark multiple messages.

Compose a message.

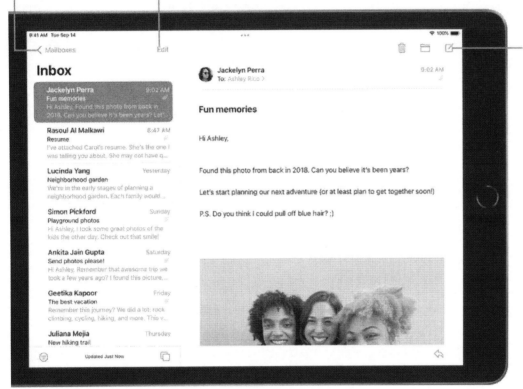

» Click on the Create icon.
» Touch the e-mail & write your message with the keyboard.

Aa

» Touch the Text Format icon at the upper part of your onscreen keyboard to make changes to the font style and text color, add italic style or bold style, add a numbered or bulleted list, etc.

Add Recipients

» Touch in the To field, then write the recipients' names.
» If you plan on sending a copy, touch Cc / Bcc field, then carry out any of the below:

1. Touch the Cc field, then enter the names of those you plan on sending a copy to.

2. Touch the Bcc field, then enter the names of the individuals whose names you do not want to be seen by other recipients.

Add Additional Email Accounts

Navigate to the Settings app, touch Mail> Accounts> Add accounts, then pick an option. If you cannot find your email provider on the list, touch Others.

Send an Email From Another Account

If you own multiple e-mail accounts, you can pick the one you want to send an e-mail from.

» In your e-mail draft, touch the Cc / Bcc button, in the Field.
» Touch the From button, then pick select an account.

Reply an Email

» Tap in the e-mail, touch the More Actions button, and then touch the Reply button.

» Type your reply and touch the Submit icon to send it

Add a Document to an E-Mail

You can upload a file in an e-mail.

» Tap in the email you would like to attach the file to, and then touch the Add

Doc icon at the top of the onscreen keyboard.
» Find the file in the Files app and then touch it to import it.

In the Files app, touch the Recent or the Browse button at the lower part of your screen, and then touch a location, folder, or file to see what is inside it.

Add a Saved Image or Video

» Tap in the e-mail you want to insert the video or image in, and then touch the Add Image icon at the top of the onscreen keyboard.
» Click on a video or picture.

Swipe up to check out more pictures.

» Touch a picture or video to add it to your e-mail.

Capture a Picture or Video to Add to an Email

» Tap in the e-mail you want to attach the video or image to, and then touch the Capture icon at the top of the onscreen keyboard.
» Snap a picture or record a video.
» Click on Use Video or Use Image to add it to your e-mail, or click on the Re-take button to take another shot

Scan a File into an Email

» Tap in the e-mail you want to attach the scanned file to, and then touch the Scan icon at the top of the onscreen keyboard.
» Set your iPad in a way that the document page can be seen on your display—the iPad automatically takes the page.

To manually capture the file, touch the Shutter icon. Touch the Flash icon to switch the flashlight on or off.

» Scan more pages, then click on the Save button.
» You can edit a saved scan, just touch it, then carry out any of the below:

1. Crop the picture: touch the Crop icon.

2. Use a filter: Touch the Show Filter Settings icon.

3. Rotate the picture: Click on the Rotate icon.

4. Delete the picture: touch the Trash icon.

CHAPTER 5
HOW TO USE IPAD CAMERA

Camera Setup

» Go to settings and then click on photos and camera to view camera options.
» To adjust the shutter sound volume, go to settings, click on sounds, and then "ringer and alerts."

How to Use the Various Modes on an iPad Camera

This is the default mode when you launch your camera app. To take a photograph in this mode, simply press the shutter button.

While your image is being captured, Portrait mode blurs the background. To use this mode, launch the camera app, select portrait mode, move away from the subject if the app suggests it, and then press the shutter button to capture the image.

Square: This mode limits the frame of the camera screen to a square, making it ideal for social media photos.

Pano: A wide angle is captured by slowly moving your device to the right, left, up, or down while following the centerline. To activate this mode, press the shutter button and move your camera slowly from one side to the other.

Video mode: You can record a video in this mode. In this mode, the shutter button changes from white to red. Press the shutter button once to start recording and again to stop recording and save the video.

Slow-motion: This records your video normally, but when you play it, it has a slow-motion effect. To use this mode, launch your camera app, select slow-motion, and record a video.

Time-lapse: This technique allows you to record videos at predetermined intervals. To use this mode, launch the camera app and select time-lapse from the menu. Then, press the shutter release button. Until you press the shutter button again, the camera will take photos at regular intervals.

How to Modify an iPad's HDR Camera Settings

When taking photos on the iPad, HDR is enabled by default. To manually control HDR, go to settings and select the camera. Then, select "turn off smart HDR." OR, on the camera screen, click "HDR" to manually turn it off or on.

Take Pictures and Videos

» To take a photo, open the camera app on your iPad, and then, when ready, press the shutter button or any of the volume buttons.
» Stretch or pinch the image or video on the screen to zoom in and out of it.
» To record a video, launch the camera app, navigate to the video, and then press the shutter button or any of the volume buttons to begin or end recording.
» To take a screenshot on your iPad, simultaneously press the top button and any of the volume buttons.
» Swipe an Apple pencil from the bottom corner of any side of your iPad screen to take a screenshot.
» To view screenshot images, open the photos app, select "albums," and then "screenshot."
» Click on the photo app to view your images.

Make a New Album

» Open the Photos app and navigate to Albums.
» Then, in the upper-left corner of the screen, click the plus (+) button.
» Then give the new album a name and save it.

How to View Photos From "My Photo Stream"

» To view photos saved in "my photostream," launch the Photos app and select Albums. Then, select "my photostream."

How to Enable or Disable "My Photo Stream"

» Navigate to Settings and select the Apple ID account.
» Then, select iCloud.
» Then proceed to photos. You can toggle "my photostream" on or off here.

Photo and Video Editing

Viewing and editing photos in the photo app:

» Go to the Photos app, select photos or albums, and then select a thumbnail.
» Then, click edit and make your changes using the controls at the bottom of the screen.
» Then press the done button.

To Cut Videos

» Open the Photos app, then select the video you want to edit and press the "edit" button.
» To change the start and stop times, move the sliders on both sides of the video timeline.
» Then, to watch the trimmed video, press the play button.
» After that, click "done" and then "save video" or "save video as new clip."

Printing Photos From Your iPad

» To begin, make sure you have an Air Print printer.
» Connect your printer and iPad to the same Wi-Fi network.
» Then, open the Photos app and choose the photo(s) you want to print.
» Then, select print from the share menu.
» Next, choose the printer and the number of copies to print, as well as the color.
» Then, select "print."

Video Options

» To access video settings, go to settings and then video.

Voiceover Video Editing

To enable or disable voiceover, do one of the following:

» Three times press the top button.
» Use the command and control center.
» Say "turn on voiceover" or "turn off voiceover" to Siri.
» Navigate to Settings and then to Accessibility. Next, select Voiceover and toggle it on or off.

How to Trim Camera Videos Using Voiceover

When watching a video, double-click the screen to bring up the video controls. Then, with the trim tool selected, swipe to the right or left to trim the video. The amount of time cut from the video is announced by the voiceover. To finish the trim, choose trim and double-tap.

How to Transfer Photos and Videos to an iPad

» Insert a USB-C connector into your iPad to import data from another iPad or iPhone.
» Then, using the USB cable that came with the device, connect the iPhone or iPad to your iPad and turn on or unlock the device.
» Then, on the iPhone or iPad, open the Photos app and choose Import.
» Next, select the photos and/or videos to import and the importation destination.
» You can import all items by selecting "import all," or you can select specific items to import and then click on import and import selected.
» You can remove the USB after the photos and/or videos have been imported.

CHAPTER 6
IPAD SECURITY

How to Secure Your iPad With a Password

Create a passcode that must be entered to unlock the iPad when it is turned on or wakes up for added security. Setting a passcode enables data protection, which encrypts the data on your iPad with 256-bit AES encryption. (Not all programs will encrypt data.)

You can also establish or change the passcode.

1. Go to Settings and then select one of the following options, depending on your model:

» Passcode and Touch ID

2. Select Turn Passcode On or Change Passcode from the drop-down box.

3. Click Passcode Possibilities to view the password-creation options. Custom Alphanumeric Code and Custom Numeric Code are the most secure solutions.

Once you've created a passcode, you can unlock your iPad with Touch ID on supported models. However, for added security, you must always enter your password to open your iPad in the following situations:

» You turn your iPad on or restart it.
» It's been more than 48 hours since you unlocked your iPad.
» You haven't used the password to unlock your iPad in the last 6.5 days, and

you haven't used Touch ID in the last 4 hours.

» A remote lock command is sent to your iPad.
» You've tried using Touch ID to unlock your iPad five times without success.
» Change the time at which the iPad locks automatically.
» Create an Auto-Lock timer in Settings > Display & Brightness > Auto-Lock.

After ten failed passcode attempts, delete the data.

After ten failed passcode attempts, set the iPad to erase all data, media, and personal settings.

Go to Settings and then select one of the following options, depending on your model:

» Passcode and Touch ID.
» Passcode 2.
» Select Erase Data from the menu.

Deactivate the Passcode Navigate to Settings and then select one of the following options, depending on your model:

» Passcode and Touch ID.
» Password 2.
» Select Turn Passcode Off from the drop-down menu.

Password Reset

If you enter the wrong passcode six times in a row, your device will be locked and you will receive a message stating that the iPad is disabled. If you forget your passcode, you can use a PC or recovery mode to wipe your iPad and reinstall it. (Note: If you backed up your data and settings to iCloud or your computer prior to forgetting your passcode, you can restore them from the backup.)

How to Set Up Face ID on an iPad

You can securely unlock your iPad, authorize purchases and payments, and sign in to a variety of third-party apps by simply looking at it. To use Face ID, you must also create a passcode on your iPad.

Change Your Appearance or Configure Face ID

If you did not initially set up Face ID on your iPad, go to Settings > Face ID & Passcode > Set up Face ID and then follow the on-screen instructions.

If you have physical limitations, you can select Accessibility Options when configuring Face ID. Face recognition can be set up in this manner without requiring the entire range of head motions. Face ID is still secure, but it requires a more consistent way of seeing the iPad.

Face ID has an accessibility feature if you are blind or have low vision. Go to Settings > Accessibility > Face ID & Attention and turn off Require Attention for Face ID.

Temporarily Disable Face ID

Face ID on your iPad can be temporarily disabled in the following ways:

1. Press and hold the top and volume buttons at the same time for two seconds.

2. When the sliders appear, press the top button to lock the iPad immediately.

3. If you do not touch the screen for a minute or more, the iPad will automatically lock. When you use your passcode to unlock your iPad, Face ID is reactivated.

How to Set Up Touch ID on an iPad

»   Use Touch ID to securely and quickly unlock an iPad without a Home button, authorize purchases and payments, and sign in to a variety of third-party apps.
»   Before you can use Touch ID on your iPad, you must first set up a password.

How to Turn On and Off Fingerprint Recognition

1. Go to Settings > Touch ID & Passcode if you did not enable fingerprint recognition when you first set up your iPad.

2. Select one of the options and follow the on-screen instructions.

3. After enabling iTunes and the App Store, you'll be prompted for your Apple ID password when you make your first purchase from the App Store, Apple Books, or the iTunes Store. Touch ID will be required for your next transaction.

How to Insert a Fingerprint

You can enter an infinite number of fingerprints (both of your thumbs and forefingers, for example).

1. First, navigate to Touch ID & Passcode > Settings.

2. Select Add a Fingerprint from the drop-down menu.

3. Comply with the on-screen instructions.

How to Name a Fingerprint or Erase It

1. First, navigate to Touch ID & Passcode > Settings.

2. If you have a large collection of fingerprints, you can identify each one individually by doing one of the following:

    » Place your finger on the iPad's top button.

3. Tap the fingerprint, then name or erase it (for example, "Thumb").

Disable Touch ID

» Disable one or more settings under Options > Touch ID & Passcode.

Include Your iPad in the Find My iPad App

» Before you can use the Find My app to track down a misplaced iPad, you must first link it to your Apple ID.

» If you add your iPad to Find My, you'll receive a notification if you forget it.

Include your iPad

1. Go to Settings > [your name] > Find My on your iPad. If prompted, sign in with your Apple ID. If you don't have an Apple ID or have forgotten your password, select "Don't have an Apple ID or have forgotten your password?" and follow the on-screen instructions.

2. Enable Find My iPad by tapping on it.

3. You can also switch between the following options:

» Find My network: If your device is not connected to Wi-Fi or cellular service, Find My may try to find it using the Find My network.
» Notify Last Position: If your device's battery charge level falls dangerously low, Apple will quickly send you its location.

NB: Activation Lock is a feature on the iPad that prevents unauthorized users from activating and using your device even if it is removed.

Best practices for keeping your Apple ID as secure as possible:

» Never share your Apple ID with anyone, including family members. (Note: If you ever lose access to your account, you can designate one or more Account Recovery Contacts to assist you in regaining access.)
» Purchases, subscriptions, and a family calendar can be shared without sharing Apple IDs.
» Never give anyone else your password, security questions, verification codes, or recovery key. This information will never be requested by Apple.
» Look for the lock sign in the address bar of your Apple ID account page in Safari or another web browser to ensure that your session is secure and safe.
» If you're using a public computer, make sure to sign out when you're done to prevent others from accessing your account.
» Be wary of phishing scams. Avoid clicking on links in suspicious emails or text messages, and don't give out personal information on any website you're not sure about.
» Use different passwords for different internet accounts.

CHAPTER 7
IPAD ADVANCED FEATURES

Airdrop

To share an item, open it and press the Share button, Share, AirDrop, More choices button, or any other button that displays the app's sharing options.

Tap the AirDrop symbol in the row of sharing options, then tap the profile image of a nearby AirDrop user.

If the person does not appear as a nearby AirDrop user, ask them to open Control Center on their iPhone, iPad, or iPod touch and grant AirDrop access to their device. To send a message to a Mac user, ask them to allow AirDrop to detect them in the Finder.

To transfer an item using a method other than AirDrop, select it from the list of sharing options, such as Messages or Mail (options vary by app). Siri may also suggest ways to share with people you know by displaying their profile images and sharing option icons.

How to Make Use of ApplePay

Apple Pay, like your iPhone or Mac, can be used for both in-app transactions and online shopping. Look for the Apple logo followed by "Pay"—usually in black near the checkout options—for the latter.

When you select the Apple Pay option, a pop-up box will appear where you can enter your credit card information. Your shipping address and contact information will be filled in automatically, allowing you to skip all of the online checkout steps. To complete the purchase, use Touch ID.

You can use Apple Pay to make in-app purchases on your iPad just like you can on your iPhone. When you're ready to buy an app that supports Apple Pay, look for the Apple Pay option. (Note: This feature is available in a number of popular apps, including food ordering services, transportation systems, and others.)

Calendar

You can use the calendar application to manage your schedule by adding meetings, appointments, and other events. Easily create and edit events and appointments as needed. The program has an important scenario and comes with some useful features like:

Calendar Alert

If you want to be notified of a specific event, you can set up an event alert. For example, you can create an alert that sounds 10 minutes before the event starts. To set event alerts or add other information about events, tap the event, then tap Edit. You can also change this information when you create the event.

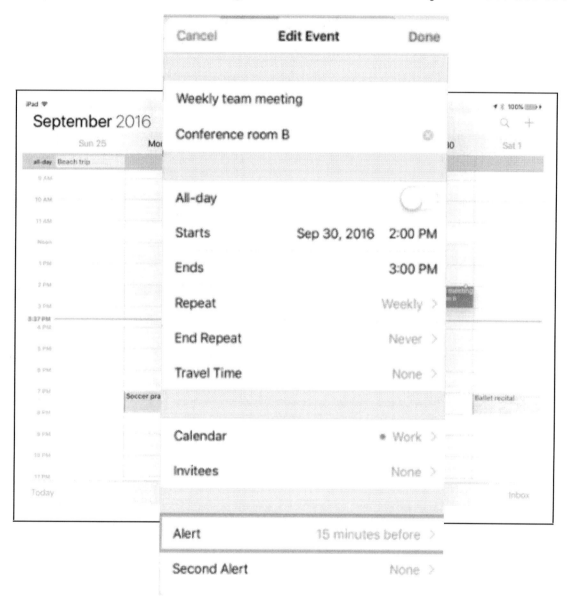

Add a New Calendar

We recommend that you create a special calendar for different types of events. For example, you can create a calendar for your work and a calendar for your personal agenda. Each calendar is assigned its own color, so you can quickly see different events at a glance.

To create a new calendar, tap Calendar at the bottom of the screen, tap Edit, and select Add calendar.

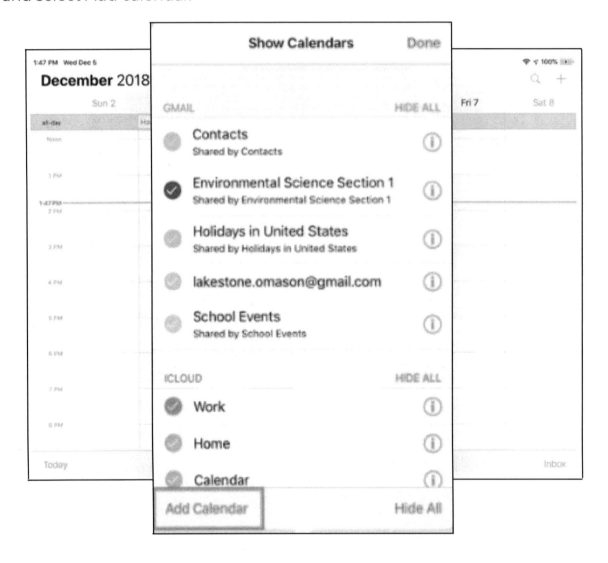

Synchronize Other Calendars

If you already have your calendar on another service (Google, Yahoo!, Outlook. com, etc.) you can synchronize it with the Calendar app. This allows you to view and edit all calendars directly from your iPad.

To add a new calendar, in the Home screen, tap Settings and Accounts in the left pane and select Add account. Follow the on screen instructions to link a new account.

From our experience, calendar synchronization from other services may not work perfectly. For example, if you have multiple calendars (for work, school, or other activities) associated with a single Google Account, they may not all sync to your iPad. When using this feature, we recommend that you keep a close eye on your calendar to ensure that it is synchronized correctly. If you need more help, you can always come back and review this chapter again.

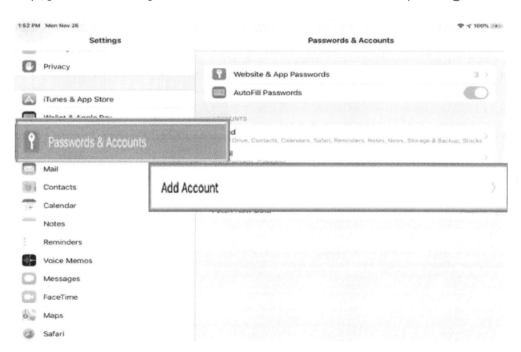

Create an Event From Another Application

The iPad will try to guess wisely when a particular text refers to an event. For example, if someone sends a message that they want to watch a movie tomorrow at 7:00, the word tomorrow at 7:00 will be underlined. Tap the underlined word to create an event.

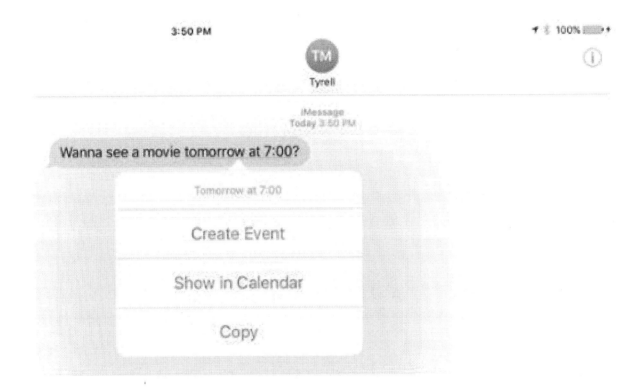

Maps

You can see your location in the Maps app.

Allow the map to make use of the Location service.

The iPad requires an Internet connection and the Location service to be activated in order for the Maps application to find your location and provide accurate directions.

If the map displays a message indicating that Location Services has been deactivated, tap the message, tap Turn On in Settings, and then tap Location Services again.

Display Your Current Location

» Select the Locate option.
» The center of the map indicates your current location. The north is at the top of the map. To display your heading at the top instead of the north, press the Heading button. To return to displaying the north, click the "Track" or "Compass" icon.

Select the Appropriate Map

The buttons in the upper right corner of a map indicate whether the map is intended for satellite viewing, transportation, exploration, or driving. Carry out the following steps to select another map:

» Touch the button in the upper right corner.
» Select a different type of map, then click the Close icon.

Look at a 3D Map

Perform any of the following on a 2D map:

» Raise two of your fingers.
» In some cities, press the 3D button in the upper right corner.
» In a 3D map, you can do any of the following:
» Change the angle by dragging two fingers down or up.
» Zoom in to see the structures in 3D.
» To return to a 2D map, click the 2D button in the upper right corner.
» Move around the map by dragging it.
» With two fingers, press and hold a map, then rotate the fingers to rotate the map.
» Examine the Earth Using an Interactive 3D Globe
» Keep zooming out till the map becomes a globe. Rotate the map by dragging it, and zoom in by pinching open to see more details for oceans, deserts, mountain ranges, etc.

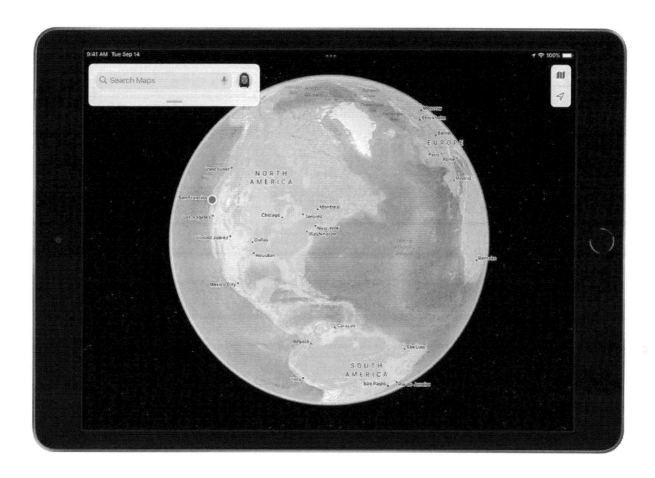

(*Find a Place*)

Click in the search box (at the upper part of the search card) then type what you want.

CHAPTER 8
HOW TO READ ON YOUR IPAD

Buy Books and Audiobooks in Apple Books on iPad

Tap the Book Store or Audiobooks button to browse titles, or type in a specific title, author, or genre to find a book.

Simply tap the cover image to learn more about a book, read a sample, hear an excerpt, or add it to your To-Read list.

Press Get to download a free title. It's as simple as tapping Buy to buy a title.

For all purchases, your Apple ID payment method is used.

Reading a Book

The cover of a book can be opened by tapping it. You can get around by following these steps:

» Changing the page by swiping from right to left can also be accomplished by tapping.
» Returning to page 1 will take you to the previous page. If you're using a smartphone, you can navigate by swiping from left to right or tapping the page's left side.

Modify the Text and Display Appearance

Tap the Appearance button, then the page, and then any of the following actions:

» Change the screen's brightness: The slider can be moved to the left or right.
» Change the font size: To make the font larger, tap the large A, and to make it smaller, tap the small A.
» Change the font: Go to Fonts to change the typeface.
» Change the background color of the page: Tap to form a circle.
» Dim the screen when it's dark: When using Books in low-light conditions, use the Auto-Night Theme to change the page color and brightness automatically. (Not all books work with the Auto-Night Theme.)
» To scroll through a book or PDF indefinitely, disable pagination and enable Vertical Scrolling.

Text Can Be Highlighted or Underlined

» After highlighting any word, drag the grab points to change your selection.
» You can select a highlight or underline color, then hit highlight and select your color.
» To remove a highlighted or underlined text, click on the desired text and then the delete button.
» Navigate to the book's contents and select notes to see everything you've highlighted.

Listen to an Audiobook

Tap the cover of a book in Reading Now or your Library's Audiobooks collection, then select an option from the list below:

» Rewind or advance: Use external devices such as headphones or car controls, or touch and hold the rounded arrows while sliding and holding the book cover.
» To change the number of seconds that skips advance, go to Settings > Books, then down to Audiobooks.
» Increase or decrease the rate: Tap the playback speed in the lower-left cor-

ner to change the speed.

» Set a sleep timer: Tap the Sleep button to set the duration of your sleep.

» Go to the following chapter: Tap the Table of Contents button to select a chapter.

» It should be noted that some audiobooks refer to chapters as tracks or do not mention them at all.

» Navigate to a specific point in time: Drag the played audiobook cover to the right. A gray circle on the timeline indicates the start of your listening session. Tap the circle to return to that location.

Change Your Reading Goal for the Day

You can change your daily reading goal based on how many minutes you want to read each day. If you do not modify your daily reading goal, it will be set to five minutes.

» After tapping Reading Now, swipe down to Reading Goals.

» Adjust your goal, then tap Today's Reading.

» Set the number of minutes you want to read each day by sliding the counter up or down.

» Books notify you when you meet your daily reading goal; touch it to learn more about your achievement or share it with others.

» To receive a notification when you reach your daily reading goal, go to Settings > Notifications > Books and select Allow Notifications.

» To incorporate PDFs into your reading goal, navigate to Settings > Books > Include PDFs.

Change Your Reading Goal for the Year

Once you've finished reading a book or audiobook in Books, the Books Read This Year collection appears below Reading Goals. The yearly reading goal is three books by default, but you can change it based on how many books you want to read.

» After tapping Reading Now, scroll down to Books Read This Year.

» Then, after tapping a placeholder square or a book cover, tap Adjust Goal.

» Set the number of books you want to read each year by sliding the counter up or down.

Enable Coaching

» You can enable coaching to receive motivation and nudges to assist you in meeting your reading goals.
» Then, in the top-right corner, select Reading Now, then your account.
» After you've enabled Notifications, enable Coaching.

Disable Reading Goals Notifications

When you reach a reading goal or begin a reading streak, you can choose not to receive reminders.

» Then, in the top-right corner, select Reading Now, then your account.
» Tap Notifications to disable Goal Completion.

Turn off Reading Objectives

Turn off Reading Goals in Settings > Books. Reading Now's reading indicators are obscured and you don't receive reading notifications while Reading Goals is switched off.

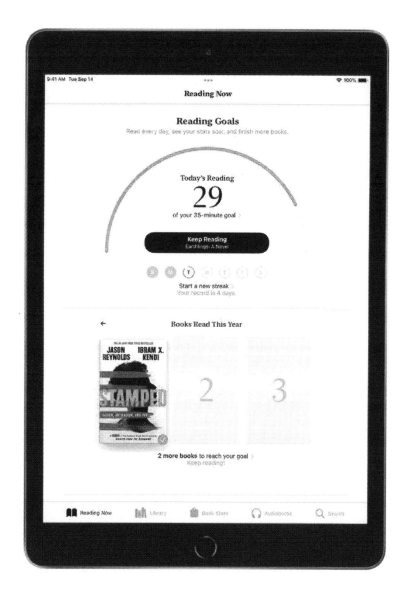

Create a Collection of Books

To customize your library, you can create your collections.

1. To create a new collection, go to Library, then Collections, then New Collection.

2. Tap Done after giving the collection a name, such as Beach Reads or Book Club.

3. To add a book to the collection, press the More Info button below the cover (or on the book's details page in the Book Store), tap Add to Collection and then select the collection.

The same book can be added to numerous collections.

Sort Books in Your Library

Pick how your library's books are organized and displayed.

1. Scroll down and tap the word that comes next to Sort or Sort By after tapping Library.

2. Select Recent, Title, Author, or Manually from the drop-down menu.

Touch and hold a book cover, then drag it to the desired place if you chose Manually.

3. To see books by title or cover, use the Table of Contents button.

Tip: The same method can be used to sort books within a collection.

Remove Books, Audiobooks, and PDFs

You can conceal books, audiobooks, and PDFs on your iPad or delete them from Reading Now and your library collections.

1. Then tap Edit, then Library.

2. Tap Library, then select Audiobooks from the drop-down menu.

3. Remove the objects you wish by tapping them.

4. Select an option by tapping the Trash button.

Tap Reading Now, hit your account symbol, then tap Manage Concealed Purchases to unhide books and audiobooks you've hidden.

Notes App

Take Notes on an iPad

» Open the Notes app, click the New Note icon, and then type the note's title on the first line.
» After that, type your note.
» When you're ready to save the note, click "done."

Making a Checklist

» Launch the notes app and then select the checklist icon.
» Then, add it to your list.

To Modify the Notes Display

» Turn the iPad into portrait or landscape mode to change the display. OR, while viewing the note in landscape mode, click the "enter full screen" button.

How to Create an Apple External Keyboard Shortcut

» To begin a new note, press command-N.
» To add a checklist, press shift-command-L.
» To see more keyboard shortcuts, press and hold the command key.

CHAPTER 9
HOW TO WATCH TV

Subscribe to Apple TV Channels

» Tap Watch Now, then choose a channel from the Channels menu.
» After tapping the subscription button, follow the onscreen instructions, reviewing the free trial (if applicable) and subscription terms.

» You can watch content on-demand or download it to watch later after you sign up for a subscription.

Incorporate Your Cable or Satellite Service Into the Apple TV App

» With a single sign-on, you can access all of the supported video apps in your subscription package.
» Under Settings, select TV Provider from the drop-down menu.
» Choose your TV provider, then sign in with the credentials provided by that provider.
» Sign in from the app if your TV provider isn't displayed.
» Then, tap Originals, followed by the Subscribe button.
» Examine the details of the free trial (if applicable) and subscription, then follow the onscreen instructions.
» Your Apple TV+ Subscription can be changed or canceled.
» Then, in the top right corner, tap the My Account button or your profile image, and then tap Watch Now.
» Select Manage Subscriptions from the drop-down menu to manage your subscriptions.

Content can be streamed or downloaded.

Programming from Apple TV+ and Apple TV channels is available in the Apple TV app, whereas content from other providers is available in their video app.

Simply tapping an item will bring up more information about it.

Choose one of the following options (not all options are available for all titles):

The following methods can be used to watch Apple TV+ or Apple TV channels: Now play the video. If you aren't already a subscriber, tap Try It Free (available for qualified Apple ID accounts) or Subscribe if you aren't already.

Select a different video app: If the title is available in multiple apps, go to How to Watch and choose one.

Download: From the drop-down menu, choose Download. Even if your iPad isn't connected to the internet, you can access the downloaded item through your library.

Watch Sports

Tap Sports in the sidebar, then select an option from the list below:

» Current and upcoming games can be found in the top row.
» Scroll down to find football, baseball, basketball, and other sports.
» Scroll down to the Browse row and select a sport to narrow your search.

View a Live Game

After you've decided on a game, click Live Now. Alternatively, go to How to Watch and choose an app from the drop-down menu.

The current score and play-by-play updates for some games may be available on the game page.

To hide live game scores, go to Settings > TV and deactivate Show Sports Scores.

CHAPTER 10
SIRI AND APPLE MUSIC

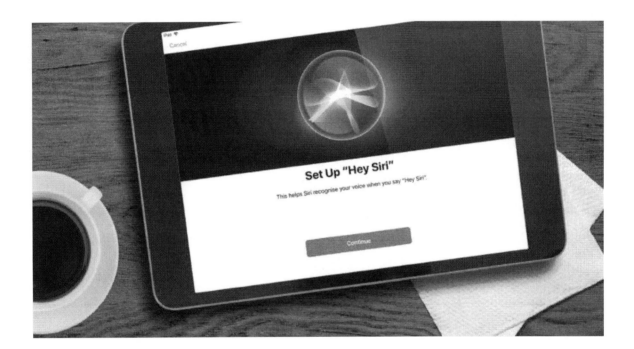

How to Configure Siri on iPad

» Go to settings and then click on "Siri and search"
» Next, if you want to activate Siri with voice, then enable "detect 'Hey Siri'".

» If you want to activate Siri with a button, click on "press top button for Siri" on your iPad.

Performing a Task With Siri

» To ask Siri to perform a task, say "Hey Siri" to activate Siri and then ask your question or give your instruction. Or, click and hold the top button to activate Siri and then when Siri appears, give your instruction or ask your question.
» Note: to prevent your iPad from responding to "Hey Siri", place the screen of your iPad on its face down. Or go to settings and then click on "Siri and search". Next, click on deactivate and then turn off "detect 'Hey Siri'"

Writing to Siri

To write to Siri instead of speaking,

» Go to settings and then click on Accessibility.
» Next, click on Siri and then turn on "write to Siri"
» To make a demand, activate Siri by pressing and holding the top button and when Siri appears, use the keyboard to type your question or instruction.

How to Change Siri's Language

» Go to settings and then click on "Siri and search".

On the right side of the screen, click on "language" and then choose your desired language.

Music App

How to Listen to Music With Your iPad

Apple Music is Apple's streaming music service, similar to Spotify, Amazon Music Unlimited, Google Play Music, and Tidal, with the advantage of lossless audio and support for Spatial Audio.

Apple Music has nearly 75 million songs in its catalog. The material, along with the selected Beats 1 radio station, is available for streaming or offline listening. There are more song- and genre-specific radio stations available.

Apple Music integrates with your existing iCloud Music Library, allowing you to keep both Apple Music and iTunes music in one place.

How to Configure Apple Music

One of Apple Music's most appealing features is its ability to adapt to your interests and preferences through suggestions and personalized playlists.

Choosing Artists and Genres

After completing the initial membership process, the next step is to select the music genres you want to listen to.

On the screen, a series of bubbles representing various genres will appear. Tap or click on those you admire and double-tap or click on those you prefer. If you don't like a particular genre, you can also press and hold it. If you make an error, you can restart by pressing the reset button.

After completing the assignment, you will be required to perform the same piece for one of your favorite performers. It's worth noting that the more time you spend on these setup screens customizing your settings, the more personalized Apple Music will become once you start using it. You will not be able to interact with the bubble displays again, so if you want quick and accurate guidance, take your time.

How to Find New Podcasts

» To find a podcast, use the search bar at the bottom of the screen.
» To listen to an episode, go to the podcast and then to the episode.
» Swipe left on an episode and then click the download icon next to it.
» To subscribe to a podcast, go to "featured podcasts" or "top charts," then find the podcast you want and click "Subscribe."
» To remove or delete a downloaded episode, go to Library and then Episode. Then, on the episode, swipe left and then click "remove download" or "unsaved."
» To delete all downloaded episodes, go to "Library" and then "Downloaded." Then, click the three dots (...) and then "Remove all downloads."
» To share a podcast or episode, go to "Library" and then to the episode's information page. Then, in the top-right corner of the screen, click the three dots (...) and select "share show."
» To share an episode, click the three dots next to the episode, then click "share episode."

CHAPTER 11
ACCESSIBILITIES ON YOUR IPAD

Translate Text or Your Voice

After selecting the languages to be translated, select one of the following options:

» Before pressing Go, tap "Enter text" and type a phrase.
» Then, after pressing the Listen button, speak up.

When the translation appears, choose one of the following options:

» Play the translation's audio version: To get started, press the Play button.
» Take note of the translation and save it to your favorites: From the drop-down menu, choose Favorite.
» Look it up in the dictionary: To see a word's definition, tap it first, then the Dictionary button.
» Show another person how to translate: Press the Enter Full-Screen button to go full screen.
» Swipe down on the translation to learn about your recent activities.

A conversation can be translated. From the drop-down menu, choose Conversation.

Select one of the two languages to speak after pressing the Listen button.

It is possible to translate a conversation without first pressing the microphone icon. To begin the conversation, select More Options, then Auto Translate, and finally Listen. The iPad detects when you start and stop speaking.

When you're talking face to face, tap the Conversation View button, then Face to Face to see the conversation from each person's point of view.

Languages can be downloaded for offline translation or on-device translation.

You can download languages to translate when you don't have internet access or On-Device Mode is enabled.

Under Settings, select Translation from the drop-down menu.

Tap Downloaded Languages, then the Download button next to the languages you want to download.

On-Device Mode must be enabled.

Text Translation Apps

You can translate any text in apps like Safari, Messages, Mail, compatible third-party apps, and others. When typing text on your iPad, you can even replace what you wrote with a translation.

After selecting the text to be translated, tap Translate.

You can choose from the options listed below the text translation:

Translation should be used in place of the original content (available only when entering text).

Copies and pastes the translation into a different application, such as a second one.

The language of the original text and its translation are both editable in any of the available languages.

This item has been added to your favorites list. The Translate app saves your preferred translations.

Use the Translate app's translation capabilities.

What you see through the camera should be translated. Adjust the iPad's position so that the text appears after you launch the Camera app.

When the yellow frame around the discovered text appears, tap the Detect Text button.

After you've chosen the text to be translated, tap Translate.

Enable Screen Time

Before you can view your app and device usage, you must first enable Screen Time.

Screen Time can be found in the Settings menu.

» Tap Turn On Screen Time, then Continue to enable screen time.
» Tap This is My iPad if you're configuring Screen Time on your iPad for yourself.
» Tap This is My Child's iPad if you're configuring Screen Time for a child (or another family member).

To use Screen Time on all of your Apple devices, scroll down and select Share Across Devices.

Check Out Your Screen Time Report

After you enable Screen Time, you can view a report on your device usage that includes details like how much time you spend using specific types of apps, how frequently you pick up your iPad and other devices, and which apps send you the most notifications.

Navigate to Settings > Screen Time to do so.

To view a summary of your weekly or daily usage, tap See All Activity, then Week or Day.

Screen Time Should Be Used on All Devices

To share your Screen Time settings and reports across all of your devices, make sure they're all signed in with the same Apple ID and that Share Across Devices is turned on.

Screen Time can be found in the Settings menu.

Scroll down to the section Share Across Devices and turn it on.

Plan Time Away From the Screen

Screen Time allows you to turn off apps and notifications when you want to disconnect from your devices. You could, for example, schedule downtime before meals or before going to bed.

» If you haven't already, go to Settings > Screen Time and enable it.
» Tap the Downtime button to enable it.
» Select Every Day or Customize Days, then enter the start and end times.

Set App Usage Limits

» If you haven't already done so, go to Settings > Screen Time and enable it.
» Go to App Limits and then Add Limit to add a limit.
» From the drop-down menu, select one or more app categories.
» To set individual app restrictions, click the category name to see all of the apps in that category, then select the apps you want to limit. If you select multiple categories or apps, the time limit you specify will apply to all of them.
» Then, select Next and enter a time limit.
» Tap Customize Days, then set restrictions for specific days to choose a time limit for each day.
» When you're finished setting restrictions, tap Add.

Set App and Downtime Limits on a Family Member's Device

» On your family member's device, go to Settings > Screen Time.
» Select Screen Time, then Continue, and finally, This is My Child's iPad.
» Enter the start and end times, then click Set Downtime to configure your family member's downtime (time away from the screen).
» Select the categories you want to manage to set restrictions for the apps you want to manage (for example, Games or Social Networking).

» To view all of the categories, select Show All Categories.
» Set a time limit by tapping Set, then Set App Limit.
» Tap Continue, then enter a Screen Time passcode to manage your family member's Screen Time settings.

Get a Report on Your iPad's Device Usage

In the Settings menu, select Screen Time. Select one of the following options after tapping View All Activity:

» Tap Week to see a summary of your usage for the week.
» Tap Day to see a summary of your daily activities.
» Helpful Touch
» To enable assistive touch, go to settings and then general. Next, select Accessibility and then assistive touch.
» To change the tracking speed when using an accessory (such as a joystick), go to settings and select general. Navigate to Accessibility, then Assistive touch and touch speed.
» Drag the menu button anywhere along the screen's edge to reposition it.
» Simply click anywhere on the screen to exit the menu without performing a gesture.
» Go to settings, then general, to create your own gesture. Then, go to Accessibility, select Assistive Touch, and then "create new gesture." Alternatively, click the menu button and then favorites. Then, on an empty gesture placeholder, click.
» Click on the menu and then on the device to perform a multi-finger swipe or drag gesture. Then, select "more" and then "gestures." Enter the number of digits required for that gesture now. When a circle appears on the screen, swipe or drag it to the desired direction for the gesture, and then tap the menu button.

CHAPTER 12
IPAD ACCESSORIES

Airpods and Earpods

Airpods have become one of the essential accessories for Apple devices in the past few years. They are typically headphones but with wireless technology. Airpods provide high-quality sound and a flawless microphone that can make calls. They connect to your device using Bluetooth technology.

To connect to Airpods from your device, head over to Settings>Bluetooth and turn on the Bluetooth. Without Bluetooth, it is not possible to connect your Airpods.

Now, head over to the home screen and open your Airpods case for the iPad to detect your Airpods automatically. A graphic pop-up will appear on your home screen. Click on the "Connect" button on this pop-up to automatically pair Airpods to your iPad.

If you don't have Airpods, you can also use EarPods that come with a headphone jack or lightning connector to listen to music. All you have to do is insert your EarPods connector into the slot to make the iPad use it as output.

Apple Pencil

The second-generation Apple Pencil now supports gestures, so you can switch brushes or quickly switch from a brush to an eraser without picking up the pen and selecting a different tool.

Apple Pencil is compatible with first-party and third-party apps on iPad. It is possible to track extreme accuracy and perceptible experience possible through third-party comparisons.

Side point detection creates shadows when Apple Pencil is tilted, and pressure support lets you draw thinner and thicker lines by increasing pressure on the iPad screen.

Scribble

Using Scribble can be difficult if you make mistakes or if the iPad doesn't save your words correctly.

Luckily, Apple thought about that and created a few gestures you can use to make your experience easier.

You can select words, delete them, separate them or join them with just a few gestures. First, make sure Scribble is enabled by following the final steps. So try these gestures.

- » Fortunately with your Pencil, you are not required to· to erase text; basically cross out the words you need to erase with the Pencil.
- » To pick a sphere of text nearby the word or expression you would need to pick. Assuming you did it accurately, you will see the featured words.
- » To input text, long press the place you need to add a word. Your device will make a space between the words in your sentence. Input the word you need to include.

To join or separate words, you really want to define an upward or vertical line between the words you need to include or in the word you need to part.

Quick Note Feature

Use the Notes application to easily jot things or create detailed info with checklists, pictures, site links, docs, etc.

Create and Edit a New Note

» Touch the Compose button, and start to type.

» Touch the Format button to change the format.

You can utilize the bold or italic font, a numbered list, etc.

» Touch the "Done" button to save your note.

To add a checklist to a note, just touch the check-list button then start writing. Press the return button to enter the next item. Swipe to the right or left on an item to decrease or increase the item's indentation

To add a table to a note, simply touch the Table button. To insert text, just touch a cell, then start typing. Press & hold the shift button and touch next to enter another line. To remove a table & change a table's content to normal text, tap

on a cell in the table, click on the Remove Table button, then click on the Convert to Text button.

Apple Keyboard

Magic Keyboard for iPad

Like the iPad Pro, the Magic Keyboard, due out in early 2020, is designed to work with the iPad Air. The Magic Keyboard is a beautiful cover that includes a fully backlit keyboard and trackpad for the first time.

Magic Keyboard uses the mechanical properties of the MacBook Air and MacBook Pro.

The Magic Keyboard is iPad Air compatible and can be used to create a magnetic connection with access to a desktop and laptop. The viewing angle can be adjusted to a temperature of up to 130° thanks to the hinges, allowing it to be adapted to any situation. The Magic Keyboard is designed to "levitate" the iPad in the light when in keyboard mode, with the lower part of the case tilted backward.

The folio design of the keyboard protects the iPad Air by covering both the front and back of the device when not in use. The Magic Keyboard includes a USB-C port for pass-through USB-C inductive charging, freeing up the built-in USB-C port on the iPad Air for peripherals such as external drives and displays.

iPad Smart Keyboard

Magic Keyboard is not available on all iPad models. Apple offers the Smart Keyboard Folio as an alternative for iPad Air and basic iPad models. It performs similarly to the Magic Keyboard but lacks a trackpad.

Make sure your Bluetooth is turned on before connecting to the Smart Folio Keyboard. To pair the Smart folio keyboard with the device, go to Settings > Bluetooth and select it.

Apple Trackpad and Mouse

A trackpad and keyboard are required for a complete office setup. All iPad models come with excellent trackpads from Apple.

Make sure your Magic Trackpad is charged and turned on before connecting. Go to Settings, turn on Bluetooth, and search for new devices to pair with the device.

Some Magic Trackpad Gestures

- » To click, press the trackpad once.
- » To hold, press the trackpad once and hold it with one finger.
- » To drag and move, click once on the trackpad and hold it while sliding your finger across it.
- » If the Magic Keyboard is locked, tap it once to wake it up.
- » Swipe to the bottom of the screen with one finger to return to the home screen from any application.
- » Swipe your hand to the top right to open the control center.
- » Swipe your hand to the top left to open the notification center.
- » Swipe three fingers left or right to switch between apps.
- » Use the pinch gesture with your fingers to zoom in on any images or maps.
- » While the trackpad offers more gestures for iPad users, you can still perform many tasks on your iPad with a regular wireless mouse.
- » To connect an iPad mouse, go to Settings>Bluetooth and connect to the mouse. Once connected, you can control your iPad with simple gestures like click and double-click.
- » Aside from Apple's official accessories, you can connect to third-party accessories such as wireless headphones and controllers via the Bluetooth option in Settings.

Charger for Lightning

Some iPad chargers, believe it or not, charge faster than others. At this point, the distinction is directly related to watts. Basically, the higher the wattage of the charger you plug into the wall, the faster it will charge, so look for a more powerful option.

How much power is there? Aside from being discovered, a standard iPhone charger provides around 5W, whereas an iPad charger provides 12W. Apple now has a 30W wall charger available.

However, there is a requirement at this location.

Your iPhone or iPad will eventually reach the maximum power limit that it can support at one time. This is controlled by a connector/adapter on the iPhone or iPad, not by the charger.

Meanwhile, if you're carrying a laptop, this could cause issues. Typical USB ports on laptops or computers provide around 2.5W.

If faster charging is a priority, use an iPad charging cable connected to a power source and a more powerful charger.

Charger for USB-C

The options for iPads that use USB-C expand even further. Essentially, USB-C is touted as much faster charging, but the speed is also dependent on the power of the charger that is plugged into the outlet.

When it comes to charging a laptop, the USB-C output will most likely charge your iPad faster than the standard USB. This is because USB-C supports USB 3.1 speeds, whereas standard USB chargers only support USB 2.0.

CHAPTER 13
TRICKS AND TIPS FOR YOUR IPAD

Use Text Shortcuts

If you frequently use the same blocks of text, make them text replacements in Settings > General > Keyboards. You can use this to create shortcuts, such as a semicolon followed by "sorry" to automate polite responses to product presentations.

Make Use of Emoji

To use emojis, simply tap the smiley button in the lower left corner of your iPad's on-screen keyboard; to return to normal mode, tap ABC. What, no grins? Navigate to the Settings section, then to General, then to Keyboards, and finally to Add a Fresh/New Keyboard and select an Emoji from the list.

The Keyboard Is Drifting

The standard iPad console takes up a lot of space, especially in scene mode. To limit it, snap on and hold the console/keyboard image at the bottom left of the keyboard/console, then slide to Float. The console is now much more compact, and you can reposition it by dragging its base edge. Squeeze it with two fingers to restore it to its normal size.

Transmission Using AirPlay

If you have an AirPlay-enabled device - such as an Apple TV or an AirPlay speaker - you can stream movies and music from your Air device by tapping the AirPlay icon in Control Center. If your device does not support AirPlay but has a competing system, such as Chromecast, look for an app like Tubio, which streams everything in full HD.

Consider Photography

This is also applicable to the iPhone: You'll hear a click if you simultaneously press the Home and Sleep/Wake buttons (or the Power and Volume Up buttons if you don't have a Home button). The screenshot is automatically saved to your photo library, but for a brief moment, a thumbnail appears on the screen: tap it to edit it before saving or sharing it.

Display Two Applications at the Same Time

Slide Over is compatible with iPads starting with the iPad Air/iPad mini 2 and allows you to quickly switch to another app without leaving your current one. For faster switching, your iPad remembers the apps you use in this mode. To use it, unwrap the first application and dash upwards from the bottom to reveal the Dock.

Long press the second application symbol to bring it up; it will now appear in its own board/panel. If you unwrap an app while you're already in Split View mode (more on that later), drag it over the splitter between the two open apps.

Use Gestures for a Variety of Tasks

In iPadOS, there are numerous motions. Squeeze with four or five thumbs in an app to see the running applications; swipe to the side with the same fingers to switch between open apps. If you keep accidentally activating them, you can disable them in Configuration > General > Multitasking

In Split View, you can use two apps at the same time.

Split View is available on the iPad Air 2, iPad Air 4, and newer iPads, and it's fantastic: you can work in two apps simultaneously, for example, pages next to Safari while you search and write.

It works similarly to Slide Over, but instead of dragging the second application over the primary or first, you drag it from the dock to the right side of the display screen. When you enable it, your applications should appear side by side.

Apple obviously prefers that you use iCloud for everything, but a significant number of us prefer Gmail and Google Calendar. Don't be concerned: Settings > Calendar > Accounts guides you step by step through the process of adding Google Calendar, while Settings > Mail does the same for Gmail.

While Doing Something Else, Watch Videos

When you're watching a movie or making a FaceTime video call in full screen mode, you'll notice a small screen icon with an arrow; for example, if you're watching a video on Apple Music, it's by the nearby symbol in the upper left side of the window. Snap on it to shrink the video; snap on it again to restore it to its original size.

Make Use of AirPrint

If you have an AirPrint printer, wireless printing is simple: assuming your print-er and iPad are on the same Wi-Fi network, simply tap the Share menu in your app and select Print. Your iPad should locate the printer automatically.

Control Your Storage

Even the largest iPad takes little time to fill with photos, apps, and videos. Your iPad can be of assistance. Navigate to Settings > General > iPad Storage to see what's taking up space.

Many changes are now possible, including the removal of unused apps. This removes the application from your device while retaining its symbol and data. When you want it, simply snap it on to resume from where you left off. You can also completely remove applications that you no longer require.

Add Symbols Without Pausing

You can add punctuation marks and symbols to your typing without changing the ABC keyboard. To type the image shown at the top, dash downwards on a letter; for example, if you need a @ symbol, dash downwards on the A key; to get an interjection point, dash downwards on the comma console/key. You can also add accents for different languages by long squeezing a key. For example, if you long press A, you will see options for,,, ae, â, and so on.

App Blocking

You can enable Guided Access for very young children—or curious adults—which limits them to the current app and allows you to disable some of its features or parts of the screen.

Navigate to the Settings section, then to Accessibility, and finally to Guided Access. Once activated, open the app you want to share and triple-press the Home button, or the Sleep/Wake button on iPads without a Home button.

Using Safari's Split View

When you click a link in Safari, you will be given several options, including open, open in Background, open in New window, and so on. You can also unwrap the connection in Split View to view two pages/stabs at the same time.

To accomplish this, pull the connection/link to the far right side of the display screen and release it. The display screen will then unwrap the connection/link on the right while maintaining the original page on the left. If one side needs to be longer than the other, you can pull the divider in the center.

Using Maps to Catch a Train

Maps provide real-time public transportation information, and when you search for an address, you can choose between subways, buses, trains, and ferries.

If you select public transportation on the Route tab, you will also receive notifications of schedule changes and other issues that may affect your trip. In the United States, cyclists can also get instructions that warn them of steep hills, stairs, and other hazards.

Find a Place to Stay or Eat

Apple has improved Maps' features over the years and can now provide a wealth of useful location information, including photos, contact information, and TripAdvisor hotel reviews, whether retailers accept Apple Pay.

Control Your Storage

Even the largest iPad takes little time to fill with photos, apps, and videos. Your iPad can be of assistance. Navigate to Settings > General > Storage to see what's taking up space.

Many changes are now possible, including the removal of unused apps. This removes the application from your device while retaining its symbol and information. When you really need it, simply snap on it to restart from the point it went off. You can also completely remove applications that you will never use again.

Your Data Is Captured

Is your iPad storing information you don't want the wrong people to have, such as your secret plans for world dominance? No worries. Navigate to the Settings section, then tap Touch ID, then Password, and finally Clear data.

If ten password attempts are unsuccessful, your iPad will be erased automatically. You can also choose which features, if any, are available even when the iPad is locked.

Use The Hidden Trackpad

When you tap the onscreen keyboard with two fingers in an app like Mail, it transforms into a touchpad: as your fingers move, so does the cursor. This is a genuine benefit of document modification/editing.

Turn Off Notifications

It appears that each application requires you to enable notifications, and some of them take advantage of your trust by bombarding you with unwanted promotions/Ads. Disable them by going to Settings > Notifications and customizing app notifications as well as disabling specific apps.

Take Pictures From Your Camera or Memory Card

The iPad lacks a memory card slot, but you can use a Lightning or USB-C to SD card reader connector to transfer photos directly from your digital camera's memory card. Similar adapters that allow you to connect USB devices such as thumb drives or musical instruments are also available.

How to Reinstall Deleted Applications:

» Launch the App Store app on your device.
» On the off chance that it isn't already selected, click on the Today tab.

» To access your record settings screen, click on your round profile picture in the upper right corner of the Today screen.
» Purchased a snap on.
» Snap on My Purchases
» On the Purchased page, click the Not on this device tab.

Look through the list of purchased applications to find the one you need to reinstall, and then tap on the cloud download symbol close to it to download and reinstall it.

As of now, there is no direct way to clear app cache in iOS. For example, you may need to keep an application but delete its archives and data from time to time. Ideally, Apple will remember an equivalent choice for a future rendition of the operating system, but until then, the methods depicted above are your best options for cleaning up garbage from your device.

Make Changes to Your Audio

Earphone support is one of several notable enhancements for AirPod users, allowing you to adjust frequencies to suit your hearing. It works with standard wired EarPods, as well as the second-generation AirPods, AirPods Pro, and a few Beats earphones. Transparency mode on AirPods Pro can also be used to enhance sounds around you, including speech sounds. The AirPods Pro also includes spatial audio with dynamic head tracking, which is supported by an AirPods Pro Motion API, which will allow for new effects in fitness games and apps. Furthermore, second-generation AirPods Pro and AirPods can switch between your iPad, iPhone, or Mac (synchronized via your iCloud account) even while you're listening to audio.

Use Voice Memo Records to Organize Yourself

Voice memos now have folders, and the non-destructive recording option has been improved to reduce background noise and echo. Updates include a couple of new highlights/elements, such as more intelligent ideas and the ability to assign reminders to clients. The App Store gives a more comprehensive overview of each app's main features; oddly, it's also where you can track your achievements for Apple Arcade titles and see what your friends are playing through Game Center. The two administrations do not have their own applications.

Make Emojis Function

Tap the globe key to cycle through the international keyboards listed in Settings > General > Keyboard > Keyboards, including Emoji, as before. Previously, selecting Emoji on a hardware keyboard changed the on-screen keyboard to Emoji. Overall, iPadOS 14 includes a small emoji picker. The picker is excellent, but neither it nor the full-screen console has iOS 15's ability to browse emoji by console. There is a new option (Settings > General > Keyboard > Hardware console > Snap on the globe symbol for Emoji to change to emoticon while squeezing the globe key).

The primary way for software console clients to get the effect is to uncheck all but one option in Settings > General > Keyboard > Keyboards. While typing on a physical keyboard, a new rundown on the right side of the QuickType bar allows you to switch to emojis, unwrap the on-screen console, start transcription, or close the bar.

Remove Web Addresses Immediately

When typing a web address into Safari, press and hold the full stop key to reveal a list of domain extensions, such as.com,.co.uk, and others. We know it's a minor detail, but it saves you precious milliseconds that you might need later.

Make Your iPad Quieter

Some applications are extremely eager to play sounds whenever you do something, but you don't have to tolerate it if you don't want to.

Navigate to the Settings section and then to Sounds to disable explicit sounds, such as tweeting or posting on Facebook, and use Settings > Notifications to make application explicit changes. You can also use Settings > Sound to reduce the volume of loud sounds while listening to them with earphones.

Increase the Usability of Your iPad

Some features cause issues for some users. Some users may become ill as a result of the animation, while others may have difficulty moving or seeing.

Under Settings > Accessibility, there are numerous options for making the iPad more usable, such as changes to the way text is displayed and support for assistive devices.

When Saying In Apps, Use Punctuation

Apple's speech recognition can recognize punctuation, making dictated texts and emails easier to read. It's simply a matter of specifying which tag you want, such as "Message David."

CHAPTER 14
TROUBLESHOOTING

How to update iPad OS:

» When you're done updating your device to the latest iPadOS version, your data & settings will remain the same.
» Before updating, ensure you back up your tablet.

Update Your iPad Automatically

If you did not enable automatic updates when you first set up your device, do the following:

» To launch the app, click on the Settings app icon, then go to General, Software Update, and finally the Automatic Update button.
» Activate Install the iPadOS Update after downloading it.
» When an update is available, your device will download it overnight while charging and connected to WiFi. You will be notified before the update is installed.

How to Update Your iPad Manually

You can check for and install software updates whenever you want.

To launch the Settings app, click on the app's icon, then select General, then Software Updates. You'll see your device's current operating system and whether or not an update is available.

How to Use iCloud to Backup Your iPad

» Navigate to settings and then to your name.
» Then, under iCloud, select and enable iCloud backup.
» When backup is enabled, iCloud automatically backs up your iPad every day while it is connected to Wi-Fi, powered on, and locked.
» Click "Back up now" to perform a manual backup.
» Go to settings and click on your name to view your iCloud backups. Then, select iCloud and then "manage storage." Then, select "backups."
» You can delete a backup by selecting it from the list and clicking the "delete backup" button.

Using the Mac

» Using a USB cable, connect your iPad to the computer.
» Select your iPad in the finder sidebar, then click "general" at the top of the finder window.
» Next, choose "backup all data on your iPad to this Mac."
» Then, select "encrypt local backup" to password-protect the backed-up data, and then enter a password.
» Finally, select "back up now."

Using a Windows Computer

» Launch iTunes after connecting the iPad to the computer with a USB cable.
» Then, in the iTunes app, click on the iPad button at the top left of the iTunes window.
» Next, select "summary," and then, under "backups," select "back up now."
» Select "encrypt local backup" to password-protect your backup, and then enter a password.
» Then, select "set password."

How to Recover Data From a Backup

Restoring an iPad from an iCloud Backup:

» Turn on the newly deleted or new tablet.
» Follow the instructions on your screen to select a region and language.
» Setup Manually should be selected.
» Click the Restore from iCloud Backup button, then follow the instructions on your screen.

Restore Your iPad From a Backup on Your Computer

Connect your computer containing your backup and your iPad using the appropriate USB cord.

Perform any of the following:

» In the finder sidebar on your Mac: Select your iPad, then press the Trust button.
» MacOS 10.15 or later is required.
» On a Windows computer, launch the iTunes application and enter: If you have multiple devices connected to your computer, click the device button near the upper left corner of the iTunes window, then select the recently erased or new iPad from the list.
» Click the Restore from this Backup button on the Welcome screen, select a backup copy from the Backups list, and then click Continue.

How to Restore Default iPad Settings

You can reset all iPad settings to factory defaults without erasing your data or content. This option deletes the iPad's location settings, privacy settings, Apple Pay cards, home screen layouts, and network settings, all of which must be re-entered. However, it does not affect your data or applications.

CONCLUSION

Thank you for reading this book. The 2022 iPad comes with a slew of new features and functions to enjoy. The newly released device provides users with premium entertainment and work functions, and with the help of this guide, Seniors can master and work their way to becoming experts and pros when using the device.

Furthermore, this book covers topics such as how to set up your new iPad, manage files on your iPad, use Siri, use Find My, secure your device, use Apple Music, and much more.

Read through this guide to get into the thick of it and start enjoying your device.

Good luck.

GLOSSARY

Apple ID: Apple ID is the only account that you need to access different services offered by Apple on their devices

Accessibilities: System Settings that can help users interact with the device easily.

Accessories: Third-party or first-party devices that can help iPad users to maximize their performance and productivity with the device

AirDrop: An Apple device-specific feature that can be used to share files between different Apple devices easily

AppStore: The default shop where Apple users can download applications for their iPad or iPhone

Apple Music: The music subscription that Apple provides for users worldwide

Backups: A particular file that can be used to restore your iPad at anytime

Bluetooth: A wireless connection service that can be used to connect accessories to the iPad

Books: A default application that provides the ability to read books on your iPad in ePub and PDF formats

Clock: A default application that can be used to keep alarms or to check the world clock

Calendar: A default iPad application that will help you to create events and manage reminders

x

Control Center: An iOS utility that helps you to easily control different inbuilt controls provided by the device, such as Torch, low power mode, and Dark mode

Do not disturb: Helps you to ignore calls that are not coming from your contacts list.

Dock: Helps you to manage apps that are frequently used on your iPad

Face ID: A new authentication procedure for iPad users

FaceTime: Default video chat application for iPad users

GPS: Navigation system that is used for location sharing and Apple Maps

iMessages: A default chat application provided by Apple for its users

iCloud: The cloud service that Apple users can use to upload their data into encrypted servers constantly

iPad OS: The name of the operating system that the iPad uses

Maps: A default application that can be used to access navigation features quickly

Network connection: A way by which you can connect your device to the internet

Notification Center: An interface where you can look at your app notifications

Photos: The default iPad application to look at images and videos

Shortcuts: A default Apple application that helps iPad users to automate things

Safari: A default web browser developed by Apple to browse the internet on Apple devices such as iPhone, iPad, and Mac

REFERENCES

A Beginner's Guide to Safari on the iPhone, iPod, and iPad. (n.d.). Lifewire. Retrieved February 14, 2022, from https://www.lifewire.com/using-Safari-iphone-browser-2000784

dummies—Learning Made Easy. (n.d.). www.dummies.com. Retrieved February 14, 2022, from https://www.dummies.com/article/technology/electronics/tablets-e-readers/ipads/for-seniors-use-the-ipad-online-user-guide-205699

Never forget a thing by using the Notes app on your iPhone! (2022, January 24). IMore. https://www.imore.com/how-create-edit-and-delete-notes-iphone-or-ipad

Provan, D. (2018). iPad in easy steps (2nd ed.). Wiley.

Apple. (2022a). Apply an effect in Photo Booth on Mac. Apple Support. https://support.apple.com/en-ae/guide/photo-booth/pbhl9df7dfbb/mac#:~:text=With%20some%20distortion%20effects%2C%20a,the%20middle%20row%20of%20effects

Apple. (2022b, January 5). Connect to the internet with your Mac. Apple Support. https://support.apple.com/en-us/HT201735

Apple. (2022c). Customize your Mac with System Preferences. Apple Support. https://support.apple.com/en-my/guide/mac-help/mh15217/mac

Apple. (2022d). Get directions in Maps on Mac. Apple Support. https://support.apple.com/guide/maps/get-directions-mps4d8a6bd2f/mac

Apple. (2022e). Get movies and TV shows from the Store in the Apple TV app on Mac. Apple Support. https://support.apple.com/guide/tvapp-mac/get-movies-and-tv-shows-from-the-store-atve382f24c/mac

Apple. (2022f). Go to websites using Safari on Mac. Apple Support. https://support.apple.com/guide/safari/go-to-websites-ibrw1005/mac

Apple. (2022g). iMac 24-inch. Apple. https://www.apple.com/imac-24/

Apple. (2022h). Install purchases from the App Store on Mac. Apple Support. https://support.apple.com/guide/app-store/install-and-reinstall-purchased-apps-fir0fb69db23/mac

Apple. (2022i). Make and receive phone calls in FaceTime on Mac. Apple Support. https://support.apple.com/guide/facetime/make-and-receive-phone-calls-mchl390e9463/mac

Apple. (2022j). Make Safari your default web browser on Mac. Apple Support. https://support.apple.com/guide/safari/make-safari-your-default-web-browser-ibrwa008/mac

Apple. (2022k). Photo editing basics in Photos on Mac. Apple Support. https://support.apple.com/en-ca/guide/photos/pht304c2ace6/mac

INDEX

Printed in Great Britain
by Amazon

12593204R00088